EGYPT'S BID FOR
ARAB LEADERSHIP

EGYPT'S BID FOR
ARAB LEADERSHIP

Implications for U.S. Policy

Gregory L. Aftandilian

COUNCIL ON FOREIGN RELATIONS PRESS

NEW YORK

COUNCIL ON FOREIGN RELATIONS

If you would like more information about Council publications, please write the Council on Foreign Relations, 58 East 68th Street, New York, NY 10021, or call the Publications Office at (212) 734-0400.

Library of Congress Cataloging-in-Publication Data

Aftandilian, Gregory L.
    Egypt's bid for Arab leadership : implications for U.S. policy / by Gregory L. Aftandilian.
        p.   cm.
    Includes bibliographical references (p.   ) and index.
    ISBN 0-87609-146-X : $10.95
    1. Arab countries—Foreign relations—Egypt.   2. Egypt—Foreign relations—Arab countries.   3. Egypt—Foreign relations—United States.   4. United States—Foreign relations—Egypt.   5. Egypt—Foreign relations—1981–   I. Title.
DS63.2.E3A35   1993
327.62073—dc20   93-7449
                                                            CIP

93 94 95 96 EB 10 9 8 7 6 5 4 3 2 1
Cover design: Whit Vye

CONTENTS

PREFACE

The end of the Cold War has created new challenges
for U.S. policymakers who deal with the developing
world. On the one hand, they are facing pressures at
home to scale back foreign aid in order to devote
more resources to domestic needs; on the other
hand, anxious governments are pressing them to
continue economic and political assistance because
of these countries' own economic problems and perceived security needs. In the U.S.-Egyptian relationship, matters are even more complicated because, in
addition to the factors mentioned above, Egypt is
aspiring to regional leadership and is trying to protect itself from Islamic political activists who see a
world with one superpower—the United States—as
a threat to their own interests and those of the Muslim world as a whole.

Egypt is one of the closest allies of the United
States in the Middle East and the second largest
recipient of U.S. foreign aid. The two countries have
extensive bilateral relations, which developed at a
time when both Egypt's position in the Arab world

---

and the international power-political scene were markedly different from what they are today. At the present critical juncture, it behooves American policymakers—and other students of the region—to take a hard look at how and why Egypt is pursuing a more prominent role in Arab affairs, and to discern how this dynamic will affect U.S. foreign policy priorities in the years ahead.

I researched and wrote this monograph while spending the 1991–1992 academic year as an International Affairs Fellow at the Council on Foreign Relations. I am grateful to many on the Council's staff for their assistance during that period. In particular, I would like to thank Tony Dunn and Elise Carlson Lewis for their continuing encouragement and support, Nicholas X. Rizopoulos and the Foreign Policy Roundtable seminar group for their many helpful editorial comments and suggestions, and Ambassador Richard W. Murphy for his valuable insights on Arab politics. Several academics, including Ian Lustick of the University of Pennsylvania, also provided helpful suggestions. I also thank my colleagues in the Department of State (in Washington and at posts abroad) who helped make my research trip to the region in February 1992 a fruitful one, and numerous Middle Eastern government officials and academics who graciously allowed me interviews.

Gregory L. Aftandilian

CHAPTER 1

INTRODUCTION

After years of ostracism in the Arab world because of its peace treaty with Israel, Egypt has returned to a prominent role in Arab affairs and is making a bid for regional leadership. Since the late 1980s, Egypt has completed the process of restoring relations with all Arab states, moved the Arab League headquarters back to Cairo, and worked to ensure that an Egyptian was elected the League's secretary-general. In the international arena Egypt can boast of a certain degree of prestige because of its prominent role in forging the Arab coalition in the Gulf war and the fact that the current United Nations secretary-general is an Egyptian.

The chief questions Egypt's position in the Middle East raises for U.S. policymakers are these: How, and by what degree, does Cairo's leadership quest affect Egypt's policy toward the Arab world, the Arab-Israeli peace process, and bilateral U.S.-Egyptian relations? And how do the end of the Cold War and the ramifications of the Gulf war affect these relationships?

The Gulf crisis of 1990–1991 changed the political and strategic alignments in the Arab world, and the end of the Cold War (which came at roughly the same time) helped to redirect the policies of pro-

Soviet Arab regimes. These profound changes brought new opportunities for Egypt and helped to accelerate its drive for a regional leadership role. Cairo has pursued this quest because of the political and economic benefits that accrue from it. These benefits include deflecting charges from its domestic opposition that Egypt is not sensitive enough to broader Arab and Muslim concerns, and helping its troubled economy by seeking job opportunities in, and investments from, Arab states. This book argues that Egypt's pursuit of an Arab leadership role is likely to place more stresses and strains in U.S.-Egyptian relations as Cairo increasingly demonstrates that it must give greater weight to Arab and Muslim concerns.

CHAPTER 2

THE NEW ARAB REGIONAL ORDER

The Arab world is said to form a regional system in international relations. In the words of one scholar:

> ... the Arab states share unique characteristics that go beyond shared borders or the dictates of geography and bond populations across modern state borders throughout the region. With their quasi-commonality of language, religion, social culture, economic and commercial ties, political history and self-definition as Arab states (as reflected in the foundation of the League of Arab States in 1945), these countries are more than a collection of states whose interactions are governed primarily by the fact of proximity. They constitute a regional system or order.[1]

The tumultuous regional and international events of the past few years—such as the end of the Cold War and the Gulf war—and ideological trends in the region—such as the rise of political Islam—have deeply affected the Arab system by shifting alliances within it, altering relations with outside powers, and enhancing and sharpening the debate within Arab society about relations with the Western world. There is no one Arab order today, but a system of orders, or relationships, within the Arab world that transcend subregional groupings. An understanding of these relationships, as well as of their staying power, is neces-

3

sary before we examine Egypt's leadership position in the Arab world.

THE STRATEGIC ORDER

Since the 1940s—when most Arab states began to
break away from European rule—the Arab state
system has been characterized by a struggle over
regional hegemony, with one state attempting to
dominate others or alliances of coalition blocs com-
peting for leadership. Other factors have come into
play over time, such as the influence of a charismatic
leader (Egypt's Gamal Abd al-Nasir) and ideological
impulses (pan-Arabism and socialism versus the
conservatism of Arab monarchies), but these have
been chiefly characteristics of state legitimacy that
various Arab regimes and their allies have used to
aggrandize power within the Arab system.

In the 1940s the main players in the struggle for
power in the Arab world were Egypt and Iraq. Both
states had achieved nominal independence earlier
than many of their neighbors (Egypt in 1922, Iraq in
1932), were monarchical regimes backed by the
British (hence each thought that Britain would favor
its bid for regional leadership), and believed that
historical factors[2] made them natural contenders
for regional hegemony. During this period Iraq al-
lied with Jordan, its fellow Hashemite[3] regime to its
west, alarming both Egypt and Saudi Arabia, which
forged their own alliance as a counterweight. Both
blocs vied for the support of Syria, which more often
than not sided with Egypt and Saudi Arabia to avoid
being under the dominance of its contiguous neighbors.[4] These blocs lasted well into the 1950s.

In 1958 Egypt and Syria formed the United Arab Republic (UAR). The impetus for Egypt's union with Syria was ostensibly ideological (Nasir's espousal of pan-Arabism and his support among Baathist elements in Syria who believed union would preclude a communist takeover), but the union put Iraq and Jordan on notice that the UAR was a force to be reckoned with. The Iraqi revolution by radical Arab nationalists later that same year initially offered hope that the UAR could be expanded eastward, but the new Iraqi ruler, Abd al-Karim Qasim, proved to be just as wary of Nasir as had the Iraqi monarchists. When Qasim took a strong position against the UAR, Egypt moved to improve relations with Jordan and Saudi Arabia.[5] In 1961 the UAR collapsed, primarily because of Syrian resentment of Egyptian dominance and heavy-handedness. The breakup of the UAR prompted Nasir to move leftward in domestic and regional politics, effectively dealing a death blow to Egypt's already strained relations with Saudi Arabia, which had become wary of his brand of radical Arab nationalism. By 1962 Egypt and Saudi Arabia had become bitter enemies and were locked into supporting opposite sides in the Yemeni civil war.[6]

A second attempt at the formation of an Egyptian-Syrian-Saudi triangle occurred in the years immediately before and after the 1973 Arab-Israeli war.

> [The trilateral states] had no formal agreement, but there was a clear understanding among them that they comprised a leadership bloc based on an "equitable imbalance" of assets. Egypt was the most powerful of the Arab states militarily; Saudi Arabia was by far the wealthiest. Syria enjoyed a certain prestige because of its historic role in the Arab awakening, and that gave it a degree of political influence. . . . As a team, the trilateral states were unmatched in inter-Arab politics.[7]

The alignment solidified as a result of the Arab-Israeli conflict. Egyptian President Anwar Sadat's decision to engage in war against Israel put Egypt in common cause and partnership with Syria. Saudi Arabia supported these states financially and politically prior to the war, and played a leading role in the Arab oil boycott during and after the hostilities. This alignment began to fall apart when Syria perceived that Egypt, by signing the Sinai II disengagement agreement with Israel in 1975, was opting out of the Arab military equation with Israel.[8] Nevertheless, Egypt maintained relatively good relations with Saudi Arabia until Sadat signed the Camp David accords. Saudi Arabia then went along with most Arab states in boycotting Egypt in 1979.

The Egyptian-Syrian-Saudi strategic triangle reemerged during the 1990–1991 Gulf crisis to reverse Saddam Hussein's takeover of Kuwait and his attempt to become the Arab world's strongman. Saudi Arabia needed the political support of Cairo and Damascus to condemn Iraq at Arab League deliberations and for political cover to legitimize the introduction of Western forces into the kingdom; Egypt and Syria, seeing Iraq's occupation of Kuwait as an unabashed bid to seize the Arab leadership mantle by aggrandizing land and wealth, lent political and military support to the coalition efforts to defeat Iraq. Egypt and Syria also received a windfall of badly needed cash assistance and debt relief from the Gulf Cooperation Council (GCC) states (Bahrain, Kuwait, Oman, Qatar, the United Arab Emirates, and Saudi Arabia) in return for their services in the crisis.

Soon after the end of the Gulf war, the so-called Damascus Declaration formalized the alliance of

Egypt, Syria, and the GCC states. The declaration
called for the stationing of Egyptian and Syrian
troops in the Gulf region; large amounts of economic
assistance from the GCC states, in the guise of a
special "GCC fund," to those Arab states that helped
them in the Gulf crisis (notably Egypt and Syria);
and political cooperation. However, by the summer
of 1991 it became apparent that the GCC states had
had a change of heart on the security aspects of the
declaration, and decided not to retain Egyptian and
Syrian troops on their soil. Additionally, as of late
1992, the GCC fund (which was initially touted at
$10 billion, but subsequently reduced to $6.5 billion[9]) had yet to materialize. Moreover, the GCC
states postponed a meeting of the foreign ministers
of the Damascus Declaration states several times in
1991 and 1992. The meeting finally took place in
Qatar in September 1992, but the communiqué issued at its conclusion made only vague references to
"joint Arab action." And while the communiqué
"stressed the importance of the economic cooperation" among the Damascus Declaration signatories
and called for a committee to bring "together their
states' finance and economic ministers," it provided
no details.[10] The vagueness of the communiqué was
undoubtedly a disappointment to the Egyptians
and Syrians.

Some GCC states have entrusted their protection to various Western security commitments,[11]
leading a number of Arab intellectuals outside of the
Gulf region to claim that the GCC states have separated themselves from the rest of the Arab world.
Many Arab officials and intellectuals believe that
the GCC states are still in a state of "shock" over the
Iraqi invasion of Kuwait and the outward displays

of Arab support (particularly among Palestinians and Jordanians) for Saddam Hussein and contempt for GCC rulers during the Gulf crisis. Eighteen months after the end of the Gulf war, Saudi-Jordanian relations were still strained,[12] and Egyptian-Jordanian relations were not much better.[13] Egyptian Foreign Minister Amr Musa acknowledged in May 1992 that there was "bitterness" in the Arab world because of the Gulf crisis and that circumstances were "still not right for bringing a qualitative change in the Arab situation."[14]

The GCC states' decision not to invite Syrian and Egyptian troops to their countries to form an Arab deterrent force does not mean that the Egyptian-Syrian-Saudi strategic triangle has ceased to exist. Since the 1940s, the stationing of one Arab state's military forces in another Arab state has been much more the exception than the rule. The GCC's relations with Egypt and Syria today are essentially what they were just prior to the Iraqi invasion of Kuwait: no formal alliance, but relatively good political relations. Additionally, Egypt and Syria have demonstrated periodically that they have a strategic and economic stake in the security of the Gulf Arab states and the containment of Iraqi ambitions.[15] Moreover, all of these states have an interest in making sure that Saddam Hussein is not rehabilitated in the Arab world and that Iraq does not embark on any new military adventures. Egyptian President Hosni Mubarak, while expressing sympathy with the plight of the Iraqi people,[16] has stated that it would be "very difficult to restore relations with the Iraqi ruler, especially in view of everything that has happened."[17] Furthermore, the GCC states' having opted for a Western security umbrella does not mean that they would not call back Egyptian and Syrian troops in the event of an emergency similar to the Gulf crisis. The contribution of Egypt and Syria to the defense of the GCC states during the Gulf crisis was much more political and diplomatic than military.[18] And while the GCC states, with their new Western security commitments, are now said by some political observers to have adopted a cavalier attitude toward Arab public opinion (by dropping all pretenses to Arab security), social and political pressures within their own societies make it unlikely that this attitude will last.

The GCC states are witnessing a period of less-buoyant economic times and rising domestic political pressures, especially from younger elements of their societies, who want a say in the running of their countries.[19] This younger generation of intellectuals and technocrats has developed close professional and social contacts with their counterparts elsewhere in the Arab world through university training and business dealings. As the GCC states experiment with very limited forms of political liberalization in the coming years, they will be forced at least to take seriously the views of this younger generation—who want their countries to be involved in Arab affairs and less dependent on Western security. At the same time, the reluctance of most GCC states to permit the formation of secular political parties, as well as ideological trends in the region, are moving many members of the younger generation to join semiclandestine radical Islamic organizations. While those espousing a radical Islamic philosophy would not be impressed by a regime's change of behavior on Arab security—believing that all regimes in the region have to be changed internally before there is real Islamic unity—the GCC regimes may believe that keeping involved in Arab affairs, whether by paying lip service to Arab security or by showing a commitment to the Arab-Israeli peace process, will keep younger elements of their society from moving toward the radical Islamic camp. Thus, the purported "divorce" of the GCC states from the rest of the Arab world is likely to be short-lived.

Saudi Arabia and the GCC states also have a stake in maintaining Egyptian domestic stability and Syria's active engagement in the peace process. The GCC states may believe they can afford to be somewhat complacent about instability in Algeria, for example, but not about Egypt. An unstable Egypt—with its large population, proximity to the Arabian peninsula, and traditional role as the intellectual center of Arab political thought—would be a threat to Saudi Arabia's and the other GCC states' strategic positions in the area. One scholar has described this linkage phenomenon as follows:

> Because of their shared characteristics, interactions between Arab states have tended to be intense. The behavior of individual states can profoundly affect the others, which means that these states are particularly vulnerable to regional patterns and balances, with a close and often direct linkage between regional external and internal developments.[20]

This explains why the GCC states, while failing to implement the security aspects of the Damascus Declaration, continue to fund development projects in Syria and Egypt and have lauded the political cooperation that exists between the Damascus Declaration states.[21] For example, the secretary-general of the GCC, Abdallah Bishara, stated in July 1992 that the Damascus Declaration is "an expression of the new Arab order." He explained that the declaration embodies a "political coordination process designed to secure the necessary accord and harmony in joint policies. Then there is the economic aspect, which proceeded from bilateral foundations between the declaration states, the interest in an economic contribution from each of them, and the role of economic development in consolidating the pillars of peace and security in our region."[22]

Egypt and Syria are nonetheless disappointed that the GCC states have yet to formalize agreements set forth in the Damascus Declaration. In June 1992 the Egyptian and Syrian presidents attempted to put pressure on the GCC states to follow through on some of their Damascus Declaration pledges, probably believing that by working in tandem, they would be able to push the GCC states to create and disburse the special GCC fund. At a press conference in Damascus with Syrian President Hafez al-Asad at his side, Mubarak stated:

> There are many questions posed about the Damascus Declaration. This is, as a matter of fact, because this declaration came into being when there was strong cooperation among the eight signatories. Then the pace of progress slowed. Moreover, the press continues to talk about repeated postponements of a meeting of foreign ministers of the declaration signatories. This, indeed, has confused the public a great deal. This happened in both Syria and Egypt alike.[23]

Several weeks later Mubarak, speaking at Alexandria University, hinted that formal arrangements as embodied by the Damascus Declaration might not come into being: "We will wait and see if [the signatories] implement the Damascus Declaration. To tell you the truth, I am not very interested in it because it does not make much difference to me. When I need something I talk to them. I talk to them when I am in an economic squeeze. They do not hesitate to help us."[24] In the same speech Mubarak underlined the "strong, close ties" Egypt has with Saudi Arabia and the rest of the GCC states.[25]

Concerning the Arab-Israeli peace process, the GCC states have undertaken a more active role than they have ever played in the past. They attended the multilateral talks in Moscow and Ottawa in 1991 and 1992, respectively, and have expressed a strong interest in seeing that the process continues.[26] They have also sent representatives to Arab coordination meetings on the peace process.[27] Although the GCC states are not in a position to play a leading role in the peace process, because they have historically not been engaged in peace deliberations and still harbor negative attitudes toward the Palestinians because of the Gulf crisis,[28] they would probably exert some influence with the Syrians, for example, to stick with the process should Damascus believe the process was moving against its interests. Having Syria outside of the process and criticizing the peace talks would rupture Egyptian-Syrian relations, embolden radical Palestinian groups, and scuttle the sense of pragmatism toward the Arab-Israeli dispute that has developed over the past few years—a result the Saudis and the rest of the Gulf states would want to avoid, in spite of their purported divorce from the Arab system.

THE PEACE PROCESS ORDER

The previous discussion leads us to the other major grouping in the Arab world, the peace process negotiating parties, consisting of Egypt, Syria, Lebanon, Jordan, and the Palestinians, with a support role played by the GCC states. The formal peace process is likely to last several years.

The fundamental changes in the regional and international environments since the late 1980s work in favor of making the peace process a long-running phenomenon. As many observers have pointed out, the demise of the Soviet Union ended Syria's near-term hopes of achieving strategic parity with Israel, and moved it to improve relations with Washington and take part in the peace process. In addition, the Palestinians seemed to have embraced a new pragmatism. Bethlehem Mayor Elias Freij stated in October 1991: "The Palestinians now realize that they will not win a military victory, that time is now on the side of Israel, which can build settlements and create facts, and that the only way out of this dilemma is face-to-face negotiations."[29] Sizing up the strategic balance of forces in the region, East Jerusalem Palestinian leader Faysal Husseini stated: "We are facing a stage which follows many catastrophes. The mistake we made was facing powers that were much stronger than [we]. Now new regimes have come and there is a new world order. We must understand the rules of the new game so that we can face the challenge and reach our goal."[30]

Equally important is the fact that the Arabs have embraced the peace process without having given up their core demand—namely, land for peace. Frequently citing the terms governing the parameters of the peace initiative—United Nations Security Council resolutions 242 and 338—the Arab negotiating parties can say to their own people and to their radical Palestinian detractors that they can be both committed to the peace process and angry about Israeli policies.[31] This means that during times of impasse in the peace process, the Arab participants do not have to leave the negotiations. This is essentially what happened from the autumn of 1991 until the defeat of the Israeli Likud party in June 1992.

The intensity of the Palestinian question and the overall Arab-Israeli dispute make inter-Arab coordination on the peace process a priority for the Arab negotiating states. This is the first time that all Arab cordon states and parties have taken part in a unified peace process, and the event has elicited both hopes and fears among the participants. There is hope because the United States has repeatedly stated its commitment to the principle of land for peace; there is fear that Israel will entice one of the parties to strike a separate deal and leave the others in the lurch. For example, prior to the Madrid conference, the Palestinians were apprehensive that the Syrians might reach a separate accommodation with the Israelis over the occupied Golan Heights and, therefore, neglect the Palestinian issue. In October 1991, a few days before the opening of the conference, representatives of Egypt, Syria, Lebanon, and Jordan agreed in a joint statement to "guarantee a unified Arab stand throughout all phases of the conference and the talks that complement it." A Palestine Liberation Organization (PLO) official admitted that tactical differences separated some parties, but added that "on the strategic level there was complete agreement." He continued: "Everyone gave assurances that not a single Arab state would establish relations with Israel or sign economic treaties or water projects before Israel gave the Palestinians and the Arabs what they demand. . . . Basically, that is land and rights for the Palestinian people."[32]

Similarly, the Syrians were apprehensive about the victory of Israeli Labor leader Yitzhak Rabin in June 1992, because he reportedly expressed an interest in dealing with Palestinian autonomy first, and leaving the Golan Heights issue for last. The Syrians feared that the Palestinians would be receptive to this agenda, thus possibly leaving them in the lurch. For this reason, the Syrian media insisted that any peace settlement must be "comprehensive." At the end of July 1992, following a meeting of the foreign ministers of the Arab cordon states and parties in Damascus, Cairo's semiofficial *Al-Ahram* noted that "the Damascus meeting was an opportunity for the Arab countries participating in the peace talks to declare their support for Syria and to remove any doubts the Syrian leadership may have had about the other Arab parties' position. They confirm that they will not enter any settlements without Syria, and will reject Israeli attempts to divide the problem."[33] By the autumn of 1992, the pendulum had swung back to the Israeli-Syrian track as both the Israelis and the Syrians made some conciliatory remarks and indicated a willingness to negotiate an agreement. As expected, movement in the Israeli-Syrian negotiations caused the Palestinians to be apprehensive.

The anxieties of the Arab cordon states and parties over the peace process, therefore, necessitate frequent interactions between them. The parties that want to retrieve land from the Israelis understand that their hopes could be dashed if one or more of the parties feels slighted and either opts to forget the other parties or uses radical surrogates to under-mine the leadership of the negotiators. Joint Arab action in the peace process may be accurately described as a "diplomacy of assurances," but it represents the first time that all of the Arab parties to the Arab-Israeli dispute have participated together in a peace process.[34]

THE METAPHYSICAL ORDER

Most Arab governments, including those that have had close relations with the West, were not at all happy with the demise of the Soviet Union and the end of the Cold War. They had viewed the Soviet Union as a political and military supporter of the Arabs in general and the Palestinians in particular, balancing the strong support the United States gave Israel. This favorable disposition toward the USSR extended even to those Arab states that actively suppressed their own communist movements and opposed Soviet foreign policy objectives in other parts of the world, not to mention areas closer to home, such as Afghanistan. Having correct relations with the Soviet Union also helped pro-Western Arab regimes project an image of nonalignment to other Arab governments and to their own people, who were often critical of their foreign policy positions.

In addition, the Arabs, as well as other peoples of the Third World, had a strong feeling that the Cold War rivalry between the United States and the Soviet Union worked to their benefit, not only in terms of obtaining financial and military aid, but in allowing individual states the room to maneuver politically in regional and world politics. For example, Sadat was able to move Egypt from being a Soviet ally to an American ally in a relatively short time.

This ability to take independent action was of political and psychological importance to the Arab states because of their history of being under Western colonial domination of one sort or another.

The end of the Cold War, therefore, has led to a great deal of soul-searching in the Arab world and has caused many Arab intellectuals and several Arab leaders to comment that political cooperation among the Arab states is needed now more than ever. The emergence of the United States as the sole superpower has elicited fears in the Arab world that a new "Victorian" age is dawning,[35] a reference to the late nineteenth century, when Britain was the dominant naval power and Muslims began to lose their independence. One fear is that, in the absence of the USSR, the Arab world will be forced to follow the purported dictates of the United States; on the other hand, some Arabs fear that the West, without constantly worrying about Soviet competition, will pay less attention to their concerns. This ambivalence toward the West is most evident in Arab attitudes toward the Arab-Israeli dispute. The West, particularly the United States, is often chastised for apparently siding with Israel most of the time. However, the Arabs also want the United States to remain engaged in the peace process and feel slighted when U.S. and Western attention is focused elsewhere. With the end of the Cold War, many Arabs are apprehensive that European Community matters will consume the Europeans and that the United States will turn inward to address domestic problems, thus neglecting Arab concerns. One Arab commentator stated: "The challenges are big. The Arab situation requires the Arab nation to mobilize all of its resources and to adopt the correct course to prove its existence."[36]

Also, a sense of guilt has developed among many Arab intellectuals who supported the war against Iraq. Pictures of dead Iraqis that appeared on television sets throughout the Arab world and the destruction meted out to Iraq's infrastructure during Desert Storm bothered the psyche of many of these intellectuals and led them to question U.S. and Western motives in the region.[37] When reports surfaced in 1992 that the United States and other Western powers were considering air strikes against Libya, as a result of the revival of the Pan Am 103 affair, and against Iraq, because of Baghdad's refusal to comply with Security Council resolutions, these intellectuals viewed those measures as unnecessary and unjustified Western punishment against Arabs and Muslims. One radio commentator noted that "a comprehensive issue that is widely debated today is whether the West is subjecting the Islamic world to injustice, persecution, and animosity because of its religious beliefs. . . . There are certainly some world powers that harbor animosity toward the Arabs and the Muslims and instigate the enmity of the world's major powers toward them." Castigating the United States for its policy toward Libya, one Egyptian intellectual wrote:

> What is needed now is for Arabs to forget all of our differences and relegate them to a secondary position, because the primary issue for all Arabs is cohesiveness, cooperation, solidarity, and unity of ranks in the face of Western fanaticism against Arabs and Muslims. We are at a grave historic turning point. Either we protect our existence, independence, dignity, unity, and identity, or lose all this forever and turn into another people like the red Indians.[38]

Discussion about the West's "nefarious" role in the Arab world has been a favorite theme in Islamic fundamentalist publications for many years, but recent anti-Western diatribes have also come from secular, establishment intellectuals and have been published in government-owned newspapers in many parts of the Arab world. By giving these intellectuals the space and latitude to vent their anger, the Arab governments hope to bolster their own legitimacy by demonstrating that they are sensitive to the ideological currents in the region. At the same time, however, this process of intellectual co-optation puts more pressure on Arab governments to demonstrate that they are working to protect and advance Arab and Muslim rights. Although the Arab world remains largely split because of the Gulf war, it exhibited a certain degree of unity during the Pan Am 103 controversy, and the Arab League served as a mouthpiece to voice general Arab anger over the Security Council resolutions against Libya and played a diplomatic role in trying to defuse tensions between Libya and the Security Council.

Those supporting an Islamist political ideology argue that the Arab governmental responses to the Libyan and Iraqi crises have been decidedly weak—largely because the Arab governments are not ruled by true Islamic principles, and because Arab leaders are tied to the West. Only when true Muslims, who implement the *sharia* (Islamic law), replace current regimes will the Arabs be in a position to unify their ranks and confront the West. Those who hold such views are still a minority in most Arab states, but their numbers are increasing in response to a host of political and economic problems facing the region. Various pro-Western Arab regimes probably believe that supporters of these views are beyond "rehabili-tation" and, therefore, that government policies de-signed to demonstrate anger at Western powers will not have any effect on them. However, it is possible that Arab governments hope to reach the ideologi-cally uncommitted before the Islamists reach them, and anti-Western rhetoric by establishment writers and government officials may be part of that process.

The belief that the Arab world has lost strategic ground and that the West is out to punish the Arabs and Muslims has made inter-Arab affairs on the issue of the Arab world's relations with the West more salient than ever. Arab states that aspire to a position of leadership in the Arab world must, there-fore, demonstrate that they are using the resources at their disposal to protect Arab lands and peoples.

CHAPTER 3

EGYPT'S ROLE IN THE ARAB WORLD

"Egypt, with its international and Arab weight, its leading cultural and scientific role, al-Azhar University, its Armed Forces, and intellectuals, must shoulder the responsibility for leadership, and will under no circumstances relinquish its leading role [in Arab affairs]."—President Mubarak, speaking to Egyptian legislators, April 15, 1992

"Under President Mubarak, Egypt will remain the real guarantor and the strong defender of Arab rights, regardless of the challenges."—Cairo Radio commentary, June 3, 1992

"We are helping as much as we can [in the peace process] because our position and Egypt's status in the region are basic and pivotal. . . . We cannot abandon our role because this constantly highlights Egypt's importance."—President Mubarak, speaking at Alexandria University, July 18, 1992

Egypt, a country with a strong sense of national identity and culture, is nonetheless tied to the broader Arab world by reasons of history, religion, and language. Being the most populous state in the Arab world, one of the leading centers of the Arab cultural and political renaissance of the late nineteenth and early twentieth centuries, and one of the first Arab states to achieve nominal independence (1922), Egypt has long seen itself as the natural leader of the Arabs.[1] These factors also have compelled many other Arab states to look to Egypt for regional leadership.[2] When the Arab League was formed in the 1940s, there was little doubt that its headquarters would be in Cairo and an Egyptian would be its first secretary-general.

Bolstering its case for Arab leadership, Egypt points to its Al-Azhar University (the leading center of Islamic learning and jurisprudence in the Sunni Muslim world); its well-known secular institutes of higher education, such as Cairo University; its early establishment of modern political parties; and its writers, newspapers, and films, which are widely admired in the Arab world. Additionally, several events in Egypt's anticolonial struggle—the 'Urabi revolt in 1881–1882; the nationalist revolution of 1919; the anti-British riots of the 1940s and 1950s; and the 1952 revolution, which overthrew the monarchy and led to the withdrawal of British forces—have become important components of the Arab nationalist folklore and a source of inspiration to other Arab nationalist movements.

The advent of the charismatic Gamal Abd al-Nasir as the undisputed leader of the Egyptian revolution by 1954, and a series of dramatic regional and international events—some instigated by Nasir and others that were thrust upon him—propelled Egypt to a position of Arab leadership. Nasir gained tremendous popularity in the Arab world through his decision to nationalize the Suez Canal Company in 1956; his formative role at the first Nonaligned Conference, in Bandung, Indonesia in 1955; his opposition to the Western-inspired Baghdad Pact (to draw several regional states into an anti-communist bloc); and his turn to the Eastern bloc for arms and economic assistance. In addition, the introduction of the transistor radio in the Arab world at this time allowed Nasir to go over the heads of other Arab leaders and appeal directly to the masses via his nationalist speeches. Nasir and the Nasirite political movements he inspired became a force unto themselves in the Arab world and were instrumental in projecting Egypt as the preeminent Arab state from 1955 to 1967.[3]

The Arab-Israeli conflict, up until 1967, also played into Egypt's desire to be the leader of the Arab world. Nasir and his comrades, although participants in the 1948 Arab-Israeli war, were never tainted with responsibility for the Arab defeat. As junior officers, they were considered courageous military men in contrast to the ineptitude and corruption of the Egyptian monarchical regime. Nasir emphasized this theme in his memoirs, *Egypt's Liberation: The Philosophy of the Revolution* (1955). The Israeli raid against the Egyptian-controlled Gaza strip and other events in 1955 led Nasir and other Arab leaders to believe that they needed large, competent, and modern military establishments to confront Israel at a future date. Wittingly or unwittingly, this perceived need to militarize Egyptian and Arab society helped to justify Nasir's rule domestically and demonstrate Egypt's importance to the Arabs as both a front-line state and a military power. Egypt's disastrous military defeat in the 1956 Suez war did not sully this image, since that conflict was portrayed as "the tripartite aggression" that Egypt could not possibly win, and one that Nasir turned into a diplomatic victory. If anything, the Suez war—and Israeli actions in that conflict—helped to accelerate the trend to militarize Arab society.

By the mid-1950s Egypt may not have had the most competent military establishment in the Arab world (the Jordanian army, under British advisors, probably held that position); but what it lacked in efficiency, it made up in quantities of both manpower and military hardware. Egypt also spent more on its military than Iraq, Syria, and Jordan combined. In 1958 Egypt's military expenditures were estimated at $211 million, compared with $187 million for the other three states combined.[4] Egypt used this issue of comparative military strength to project the image of being not only the strongest military power in the Arab world, but the political leader of the Arabs. In 1961 Nasir reminded Jordan's King Hussein that:

> The power of the UAR army has reached a stage which will satisfy the hopes of every Arab. If your majesty remembers that the UAR's defense budget at present amounts to $299 million, you will understand the sacrifices of the people of this republic. This fact underlines the determination of this people to undertake their responsibility towards the common enemy of the Arab nation.[5]

Nasir's revolutionary and destabilizing role in the Arab world alarmed the Arab conservative regimes, but they could not afford to alienate him entirely because of the perception in the region that Egypt played a critical role in the Arab military balance vis-à-vis Israel. In 1964, for example, the Arab states temporarily put aside their differences to present a united stand against what they viewed as increasing Israeli provocations.[6]

Egypt's disastrous defeat in the 1967 Arab-Israeli war took the luster out of the Nasirite mythology and effectively ended the era of Egyptian dominance in the Arab world. Egypt was still a major player in Arab affairs, but it used the following three years primarily to build up its own military capabilities by relying heavily on the Soviets. This de facto alliance with the USSR tarnished Egypt's nonaligned and Arab nationalist credentials.

Sadat's accession to power following Nasir's death in late 1970 initially did not alter this situation. But after consolidating power and reportedly purging left-wing coup plotters, Sadat embarked on several moves that broke from the Nasirite legacy. In a dramatic speech delivered in 1972, Sadat, with an eye toward Washington, announced that he would expel Soviet advisors from Egypt. The following year, in alliance with Syria and with the financial backing of the Saudis, he embarked on a war with Israel. According to several scholars, Sadat envisioned a limited war to achieve some initial victories to regain Arab honor and negate the idea of Israel's military invincibility. Given the state of Cold War tensions, the United States would then be forced to intervene to stop the Israeli counterattack, which, if left unhindered, would draw in the Soviets. Washington, after reassessing its position in the region, would then have to strengthen its diplomatic efforts to resolve the Arab-Israeli dispute.

The initial Egyptian victories in the 1973 war boosted Sadat's and Egypt's standing in the Arab world, and the Egyptian-Syrian-Saudi alliance that grew out of the war looked powerful enough to set the Arab agenda in the postwar period. Moreover, the Arab oil embargo and quadrupling of oil prices led to a feeling of euphoria in the region. Many Arabs believed that a new age was dawning, marked by a tremendous increase in Arab wealth, power on the world scene, and genuine political cooperation. But the disintegration of the war alliance soon dashed this headiness.[7] The alliance began to unravel in 1975, with Egypt's signing of the Sinai II disengagement agreement. A few years later Sadat embarked on a diplomatic course that would include his visiting Jerusalem (1977), signing the Camp David accords (1978), and concluding a peace treaty with Israel (1979). These policies prompted most Arab states to break diplomatic relations with Egypt and move the Arab League headquarters from Cairo to Tunis.

Egyptians of various political persuasions reacted to the ostracism with a mixture of anger and disdain toward the Arab world. The prevailing Egyptian attitude at this time was that Egypt had done more than enough to advance the Arab and the Palestinian cause. If the other Arabs did not appreciate Egypt's sacrifices, then Egypt could very well survive on its own. Coupled with these sentiments was a resurfacing of a narrow Egyptian nationalism that stressed Egypt's Nile/Mediterranean roots, as opposed to its Arab identity. The Sadat regime favored intellectuals who wrote on these subjects.[8]

During this same period, Cairo threw its lot in with the United States in the East-West struggle. After signing the peace treaty with Israel, Egypt became the second largest U.S. aid recipient after Israel. Cairo became hopeful that U.S. aid would cure Egypt's endemic economic crisis.[9] Moreover, peace with Israel would allow Egypt to concentrate on pressing domestic affairs.

Many Egyptian intellectuals and oppositionists welcomed their government's break with Moscow. Most Egyptians disliked the Soviet presence in Egypt in the late Nasir period, believing it compromised their country's independence. But many of these same intellectuals perceived Sadat's pro-U.S. stance as merely trading one superpower for another, and harbored similar concerns about dependency. Additionally, the heavy reliance on the United States and Egypt's pro-U.S. foreign policy became unsettling to many Egyptians, for whom Egypt's close ties to the West's strongest military power brought back unpleasant memories of Western domination. Furthermore, over time, Egyptians began to feel uncomfortable with their ostracism in the Arab world,[10] considering it an unnatural phenomenon because of the historic, religious, and cultural reasons mentioned earlier.

Mubarak's main achievement in the first five years of his rule was to bring a balance to Egypt's foreign policy. He restored relations with the USSR and began a process by which Egypt slowly reintegrated itself with the Arab world. This had no fundamental effect on Egypt's peace treaty with Israel and its relations with the United States,[11] though certain incidents, such as the *Achille Lauro* affair, led to a chill in relations with the United States for a time, and relations with Israel were downgraded for several years in reaction to Israel's invasion of Lebanon in 1982.

The 1980–1988 Iran-Iraq war helped to accelerate Egypt's rapprochement with the Arab world. First, it diverted attention from Egypt's peace treaty with Israel by demonstrating that there was threat to the Arab world besides Israel. Second, it allowed Egypt to come to Iraq's aid with military assistance and civilian workers. This policy improved Egypt's standing in the Arab world by demonstrating its usefulness in helping to protect the Arab world's eastern flank. It also helped neutralize Baghdad's opposition to the Camp David accords. Symbolically, this was important to the Egyptians because Baghdad had been the host of the Arab summit meeting in November 1978, which had orchestrated the Arab boycott of Egypt.

The development, in the late 1980s, of the Arab world's more pragmatic approach to the Arab-Israeli dispute (such as PLO leader Yasir Arafat's 1988 recognition of Israel's existence) and the desirability of the peace option also helped Egypt's rehabilitation. In addition, Cairo pursued a more activist Arab policy, characterized by a rapprochement with the PLO, support for an international peace conference (which the Arabs, in general, favored), and advocacy of the Palestinian right to self-determination, all of which placed Egypt more in line with the prevailing Arab consensus. By the late 1980s Egypt had essentially completed its rehabilitation in the Arab world. Syria was the last hold-out, but its fears of Iraqi ambitions, the loss of a Soviet military patron, and the desire to improve relations with the West prompted Asad to reestablish ties with Egypt in late 1989.

Egypt's reaction to the Iraqi invasion of Kuwait on August 2, 1990, can be analyzed on several levels, one of which was the personal dimension. In the weeks prior to the invasion, Mubarak had attempted to defuse tensions between Iraq and Kuwait through personal diplomacy. Saddam Hussein's assurances to Mubarak that he would not invade Kuwait, only to do so shortly thereafter, infuriated the Egyptian leader, who saw the invasion as a stab in the back.[12] On the strategic level, which is probably more salient, Egypt viewed the invasion as a direct threat to its interests in the Arab world, and one that had to be reversed.

By early 1990 Egypt viewed the Arab political landscape in a very favorable light: it had re-established relations with all Arab states, Arab radicals were in retreat, Egypt's new ties with Syria and Libya were moving along favorably, and its long-standing ties to the Gulf states were solid. In short, Egypt felt very comfortable in this more moderate and pragmatic regional atmosphere. Moreover, power was diffuse in the Arab world, allowing Cairo to slowly and steadily reassert its leadership role in the region without the opposition of a major power. The Iraqi invasion of Kuwait, therefore, posed a serious challenge to Egypt. First, it upset the political status quo: it not only gave Saddam Hussein the potential for enormous economic power, it threatened Saudi control of the eastern Arabian peninsula's vast oil reserves, whose revenues Egypt considered vital to its economic recovery.[13] In addition, Saddam Hussein's inflammatory rhetoric against Israel and his advocacy of the Palestinian cause threatened to reverse the more moderate consensus that Egypt had helped build in the region and to revive Arab hostility to Egypt's relations with Israel. Moreover, the Egyptians perceived Saddam Hussein as trying to usurp Arab leadership by portraying himself as the Arab strongman, and they believed that no state other than Egypt had the right to claim the leadership mantle.[14]

Although the Iraqi invasion of Kuwait was a threat to Egypt's strategic interests in the region, it also offered an opportunity for Cairo to exercise leadership in the Arab world, at least among those states that opposed the invasion. The emergency

Arab League meeting held in Cairo on August 10, 1990, at Mubarak's initiative, deepened inter-Arab divisions in an unprecedented fashion, but it also demonstrated to the Arab world that those states that opposed Saddam were not going to be intimidated. Despite the lack of consensus, the Egyptians and the Saudis mustered a majority of twelve states behind Arab League resolution 195, which denounced Iraq's "threats" to the GCC states and its concentration of troops on the Saudi border. The resolution then expressed support for the steps taken on behalf of Saudi Arabia's "right of legitimate defense"—namely, the request for foreign forces to be stationed in Saudi Arabia. In addition, clause 6 declared the summit members' intent to comply with the request from Saudi Arabia and the other Gulf states to dispatch Arab forces to help them defend their territories "against any foreign aggression."[15] Mubarak's strong leadership in forming the anti-Iraq Arab coalition, and the strenuous efforts by Egypt's religious and intellectual establishment to counter Iraqi propaganda, therefore, helped to scuttle Saddam Hussein's plans to turn most of the Arab world to his side.

EGYPT'S SECURITY ROLE

The defeat of Iraq in the Gulf war allowed Egypt to emerge as the strongest Arab military power, a position it had held from the 1950s to the early 1980s, when it was eclipsed by Iraq. Although the Egyptians never felt comfortable taking second place in any Arab contest of strength, they had come to Iraq's aid because they believed an Iranian victory would destabilize the region. Egypt, therefore, had dispatched soldiers to Iraq, sold Baghdad military hardware, and sent several hundred thousand laborers to Iraq to work in the agricultural and service sectors. This policy not only helped Egypt economically, it facilitated Cairo's political rehabilitation in the Arab world.[16] Moreover, Egypt's military assistance to Iraq demonstrated to the GCC states that Cairo could serve as one of their protectors, and perhaps their chief Arab protector—a marked contrast to the period of the 1960s, when Egypt under Nasir was viewed as a destabilizing force against Saudi Arabia.

The Gulf crisis, therefore, allowed Egypt to demonstrate its commitment to the security of the Gulf states. In addition to the crucial political and diplomatic support mentioned earlier, Egypt sent some 30,000 troops to Saudi Arabia[17] and participated in the liberation of Kuwait. Although Egypt's contribution to the overall military defeat of Iraq was small compared with the U.S. role, Cairo hoped to impress upon the GCC states that Egypt was their strategic ally. In light of this, the GCC's failure to follow through on the security aspects of the Damascus Declaration was all the more disappointing.

Egyptian officials, however, have not given up hope that some parts of the Damascus Declaration, including an amended security role, will be implemented eventually. In September 1991, Egyptian Foreign Minister Musa stated that the stationing of Egyptian and Syrian troops in the Gulf region is not a condition of the Damascus Declaration. But, he said, "if the situation [in the Gulf region] deteriorates again, the Damascus Declaration provides the legitimacy and the mechanism for action in such cases."[18] Hoping to allay Gulf Arab concerns about the Egyptian army—which aided the Yemeni republicans against the Saudi-backed Yemeni royalist forces in the Yemeni civil war of 1962–1967—Mubarak told a Kuwaiti journalist that the Damascus Declaration "does not mean I would send forces to any Gulf state without reason, but if any state needs it, we would not fail to do so. When an aggression was committed against Saudi Arabia and Kuwait, and Saudi Arabia asked us to send forces, we did not hesitate to do so."[19]

Egypt has gingerly criticized the GCC states for their new security commitments with Western powers and their reported desire to include Iran in Gulf security. Egyptian Defense Minister Mohamed Tantawi stated in a March 1992 interview that "the Arab countries should depend on their own security. They should coordinate among themselves to compensate for any shortage in their military capabilities. . . . Assistance from some friendly countries could be used whenever necessary and only for a limited time." Tantawi then reminded Egypt's GCC friends that "any threat to the Arab national security or the Gulf security reflects on the Egyptian security. That necessitates coordination between Egyptian, Gulf, and Arab security systems." He added that Egypt made the decision to assist in the liberation of Kuwait out of its belief that "Egyptian national security is not only linked to Arab national security, but is one of its main supports."[20]

Mubarak himself has spoken about Egypt's protective role in the security of the Arab world. Addressing Egyptian troops who fought in Kuwait, Mubarak stated in October 1991 that the "supreme" goal of the Egyptian armed forces is to "safeguard the security of Egypt and the Arab world and to maintain stability in this area of the world." He went on to say that Egypt took part in the liberation of Kuwait "because Egypt cannot renounce its principles, shun its pan-Arab responsibilities, or remain a bystander regarding an Arab commitment which emphasizes the duties of joint defense." Moreover, Mubarak said, those Egyptians who died in the Gulf war "gave up their lives to underline the fact that Egypt will always remain the bastion of security for *its* Arab world" (emphasis added).[21]

Egypt's security message to the Arab world, especially to the GCC states, is that its forces are ready to be of assistance to any Arab state that is the victim of aggression or is being threatened. Cognizant of the historical baggage of the Nasir period, Egyptian officials are carefully pointing out that they do not have designs on any state's territory. While the GCC states seem reluctant to formalize any security commitment with Egypt, Egyptian officials are still pushing the idea of joint Arab defense, probably hoping that over time, the GCC states will grow out of their Gulf war "shock" and see the political need of military cooperation and joint defense with the Egyptians.

EGYPT'S PEACE PROCESS ROLE

Egypt has retrieved all of its territory from the Israelis, but has expressed a deep and abiding interest in playing a leading role in the Arab-Israeli peace process. Egyptian leaders believe such a role will enhance Egypt's importance in both regional and international affairs, resulting in economic and political benefits. Speaking to students and faculty at Alexandria University in July 1992, Mubarak stated that Egypt is helping as much as it can in the peace process "because our position and Egypt's status in the region are basic and pivotal. . . . We cannot abandon our role because this constantly highlights our importance."[22] Egypt also believes that an Arab-Israeli peace settlement will help diminish one of the major causes of instability in the region, the Palestinian issue, and ensure that Egypt's peace treaty with Israel does not reemerge as a contentious issue in inter-Arab politics.

Egyptian officials are telling their fellow Arabs that because of Egypt's long experience in dealing with the Israelis, its close ties with the United States, and its diplomatic history, Cairo can be a benefit to the Arab negotiating parties. Foreign Minister Musa told an Arab interviewer that Egypt has a major role in the peace process "on the basis of experience, history, responsibility, and commitment." He then stated that Egypt is not a mediator between "two parties" because it is an Arab state, "but our position also takes into consideration international developments, current circumstances, and future prospects. . . . All of Egypt's power, diplomacy, and weight should be used to ensure the success of the peace process."[23]

Cairo's chief role in the peace process appears to be counsel and teacher to the Arab delegations. Shortly before the Madrid conference began, Mubarak stated: "If anyone wishes to benefit from the Egyptian experience, we will not hesitate to help."[24] The defeat in Israel of the Likud party and the advent of Labor party leader Rabin to power prompted an Egyptian government newspaper to note: "Hopefully, the Arabs have realized the usefulness of 'continuity.' Had they withdrawn from the negotiating table because of Shamir's provocative actions they would have been forced to go back to square one—undesirable by any criteria."[25]

Egypt has received some political benefits from this counsel role. Cairo has been the host of numerous visits by Arab delegations involved in the peace process, and they have praised Egypt's role and assistance. For example, after returning from a meeting in Cairo, Palestinian spokeswoman Hanan 'Ashrawi stated:

> Our visit to Egypt was part of official meetings and Palestinian efforts to promote the delegation's performance and Arab coordination. The Palestinian and Egyptian sides held an intensive seminar to review past negotiations and historical documentation and to assess the previous rounds. . . . We also discussed Egypt's role in overcoming Arab crises following the Gulf war, patching up the Arab rift, and resuming Gulf and Saudi support for the occupied territories.[26]

PROTECTING ARAB RIGHTS

Egypt is also trying to persuade the Arabs that because of its political and diplomatic experience, it can benefit the Arab world as a whole and protect Arab rights, especially in light of the dramatic changes on the world scene. A February 1992 Cairo radio commentary, entitled "Egypt's Leadership and Its Positive Actions," stated:

> The second half of last year and the start of this year saw quick Egyptian action on the Arab, African, and European levels to repel any dangers that Egypt, the Arab region, or the African continent could face as a result of massive international changes in the past few months, most prominent of which was the collapse of the Soviet Union. This collapse turned the United States into the sole superpower. It is on this basis that the new world order is being shaped. . . . Egypt's leadership had to act quickly and effectively on all fronts to

repel any dangers Egypt might face as a result of these changes, and also to ensure an effective role for itself in the regional, Arab, and African arenas and in the new world order. President Mubarak did not waste time, and embarked on a round of contacts and discussions with various leaders here and abroad to find a way to ensure Egypt's leading role in the region and to prepare for its role on the world stage.[27]

Cairo has also revived the phrase—adopted during Nasir's time—"*al-shaqiqa al-kubra* [the big sister] of the Arabs." Another Cairo Radio commentary, entitled: "Egypt's Pioneer Role in Defending Pan-Arab Security," stated:

Every day Egypt reaffirms its national and principled commitment to the Arab nation in its capacity as the nation's big sister. As such, Egypt bears a special responsibility to defend the nation's causes and security, and counter any aggression against the Arab people regardless of source. . . . Egypt's principled and courageous stand during the Gulf war enhanced the credibility of Egypt under President Mubarak's leadership on the entire international scene. In view of Mubarak's realistic and sober policy in handling all pan-Arab, regional, and international issues, the world considers Egypt today a positive and politically influential factor, whose advice must be taken in numerous international crises.[28]

The revival of the Pan Am 103 controversy in late 1991 and 1992 allowed Egypt to demonstrate to the Arabs that Cairo's influence on the world stage can protect the Arab homeland. Cairo called on the United States not to use force against Libya;[29] and the Arab League, under Egyptian leadership, issued a statement saying that it did not believe that Libya was responsible for blowing up the airliner, and urged "restraint on all sides."[30]

Egypt reluctantly agreed to abide by the Security Council sanctions against Libya that were implemented in April 1992, because, it said, it must adhere to "international legitimacy." But it allowed its establishment press to rail against Washington and the Security Council for purportedly ganging up on Libya and not allowing Arab diplomacy the time to defuse tensions and pursue mediation.[31]

The day the sanctions against Libya took effect, Mubarak stated that Egypt had pursued high-level contacts with European and American officials to avert a military operation against Libya. He also said that there had been "some harsh resolutions that were supposed to be taken by the Security Council, but Egypt intervened, and with the help of friendly countries, exploited all of its contacts and international weight to ease these resolutions."[32] In addition, Egypt allowed Libya to legally circumvent some of the sanctions—which called for severing air links, reducing Libya's diplomatic staff abroad, and banning military exports to Libya—by increasing bus routes from Libya to Egypt and taking passengers from airports near their common border.[33]

Egypt has also played a role as a "protector of the Arab homeland" by opposing the possible U.S. military air strike against Iraq in 1992 over Baghdad's failure to abide by Security Council sanctions. After two days of talks in Cairo on regional issues in March 1992, Syrian President Asad and Egyptian President Mubarak announced that they opposed the further use of force against Iraq. Asad stated: "Our concern was the liberation of Kuwait and the withdrawal of the Iraqi forces from Kuwait. This was a necessity which required military action. But I do not see that there is a necessity to take military action now." Mubarak agreed, and said that he was "against the use of force."[34] When the possibility of a U.S. air strike reemerged in the wake of Baghdad's refusal to allow a UN inspection team to enter one of Iraq's ministries in July 1992, Egypt similarly opposed the use of force. One of Egypt's government-owned newspapers stated: "We [Arabs] must tell the United States: enough war and fighting in the Gulf: otherwise, there will be a massacre, the price of which the Iraqi people alone will pay."[35]

EGYPT'S PUSH FOR ARAB SOLIDARITY

Egyptian officials have deplored the state of Arab affairs caused by the divisions of the Gulf war. Mubarak has warned:

> The Arab role as it is now is very bad. All the Arabs are losers. The Arabs are devouring one another. Foreign states from outside the Arab region will have ambitions in the Arab world. The Arabs must wake up and reassess their position in order to be able to discern their future. There must be a sound Arab vision.[36]

These same officials have also stated, however, that Egypt can help to lift the Arabs out of this morass by creating a more unified Arab system. Foreign Minister Musa explained that Egypt "has responsibility for establishing an Arab system based on stability, guaranteeing Arab countries' safety and achieving their security, and nonintervention in any Arab country's [internal] affairs."[37] Musa has also said: "All of us, especially Egypt, are working to realize Arab solidarity and to set Arab action on the correct path to realize Arab objectives."[38]

Egypt is pursuing this goal of establishing a more unified system by fostering closer relations with Syria and shoring up relations with the GCC states. Egyptian and Syrian officials, including the two presidents, are now frequent visitors to each other's capitals. Both sides have lauded the political cooperation that exists between them, a happy occurrence particularly from Egypt's perspective, which knows all too well from experience that a spurned Syria could make life difficult for Egypt in the Arab world.[39] But as one scholar has noted, the Egyptian-Syrian alignment "lacks the fundamental prerequisites of geographical and economic ties. This is why Egypt is seeking to reassert the broader framework of the Arab League. This gives Egypt a leading role in Arab politics that is not dependent on physical proximity or subject to whims of bilateral relations."[40]

Cairo is, therefore, attempting to use the Arab League, as it has done in the past, both to extend Egyptian influence in the Arab world and to foster a sense of Arab cohesion around issues it deems important. In late September 1991, the League approved of Arab participation in the peace process, marking the first time in the League's history that it endorsed an Arab-Israeli peace process without opposition. Similarly, the League played a role in trying to defuse the Pan Am 103 controversy between Libya and the Security Council, though with mixed results. To further enhance its position within the League, Egypt then supported the general Arab position that Western antipathy toward the Libyan regime should end. In September 1992, for example, the Arab League Council, under the chairmanship of Egyptian Foreign Minister Musa, issued a resolution calling for the lifting of Security Council sanctions against Libya, and emphasized that the Arab League Council "stands alongside Libya in face of the threats against it."[41]

Musa has welcomed the "emergence of Arab unanimity" with the return of the Arab League headquarters to Cairo, because "this unanimity is our only tool to deal with the new world order to protect the essential interests of the Arab people."[42] Along these same lines, Mubarak has stated that the Arab League "has an important role in coordinating the defense of the Arab issues and shaping a united Arab stand that the outside world will take into account. The more the Arab countries move away from divisions and polarization, the better prospects are for having a collective Arab stand to represent to the world as an expression of Arab unity."[43] The last sentence reflects Mubarak's sensitivity to the intellectual currents in the Arab world—namely, the need to demonstrate Arab unity in the face of the changes in the international order.

Egypt is also seeking to play a more prominent role in the broader Muslim world. It is cooperating with Saudi Arabia in sending religious missions to the newly independent Central Asian republics. The combination of Saudi money and Egyptian religious teachers reportedly will be used to "head off Islamic fundamentalism and 'revolutionary themes' coming from Iran,"[44] though the Egyptians are telling their people and the larger Muslim community that the Arab and Islamic countries are "duty bound to work with these countries."[45] Egypt's new role in Central Asia helps to strengthen its ties to Saudi Arabia and allows it to be seen as looking after the welfare of Muslims. Similarly, in July 1992 Egypt dispatched peacekeeping troops to Bosnia as part of a United Nations contingent to ensure the delivery of humanitarian aid; this measure demonstrated Egypt's sensitivity to the plight of Muslims under siege and increased Egypt's stature regionally and internationally.[46]

THE QUESTION OF LEADERSHIP

By the late 1970s Egypt was out of the Arab system, ostracized for signing the Camp David accords and the peace treaty with Israel; but no state emerged as a leader of the Arab world in the subsequent decade. A number of reasons explain this leadership vacuum. First, the traditional leadership contenders outside of Egypt—Syria and Iraq—became tied down by internal and external forces. The Syrian regime waged a violent struggle against the Muslim Brotherhood at home in the early 1980s and then was absorbed by developments in Lebanon. Iraq, which took advantage of the Iranian revolution and the sharp rise in oil prices in 1979–1980 to assert itself as the dominant power in the Persian Gulf, soon found itself bogged down in the war with Iran. Syria, meanwhile, tarnished its image in the Arab world by siding with Iran against Iraq and by battling against the PLO's Fatah wing in Lebanon. Second, the 1980s saw the development of subregional groupings within the Arab world (such as the GCC and the Arab Maghreb Union), a reflection of the Arab states' interest in focusing on matters closer to home. Third, individuals began identifying more with particular Arab states than with a generic Arab identity, hindering their allegiance to leaders outside their own state borders. Finally, ideological currents in the region were in flux, so no one leader could speak for the whole of the Arab world and find a universal Arab audience, as Nasir had been able to do in the late 1950s and early 1960s by emphasizing pan-Arab nationalism. During the 1980s secular Arab nationalism had already become largely discredited because the states that embraced this ideology failed to solve economic and social problems, as well as the Arab-Israeli dispute, but the perceived threat from the Iranian revolution and indigenous Islamists made many Arab leaders reluctant to embrace a new Islamic political ideology that would replace the quasi-nationalist and quasi-religious ideologies of most Arab states. Hence, no aspiring leader of the Arab world could claim the leadership mantle by espousing one particular ideology and succeed.

By 1990, however, Egypt, Iraq, and Syria were jockeying for new positions in the Arab system in light of the regional and international changes that had taken place. Iraq, emerging from the Iran-Iraq war, appeared to begin the 1990s as it had the 1980s, flexing its muscles in both the Persian Gulf region and the broader Arab world. Syria, smarting from the retrenchment of its Soviet military patron, was looking to improve ties with the West and achieve a rapprochement with Egypt to counter Iraqi ambitions. And Egypt, aspiring to play a more prominent role in Arab affairs, was trying to build a moderate consensus in the Arab world on such issues as the Arab-Israeli peace process, where Cairo's diplomatic skills would shine. Egypt believed that an era of Arab "pragmatism" would enable it to lead the Arab world by forging collective Arab action on unresolved political issues.

With Syria in need of Egypt's help to counter Baghdad and rehabilitate itself in the eyes of the West, Iraq became Egypt's only real competitor in the Arab world, even before Saddam Hussein's invasion of Kuwait. Other Arab states lacked the population base, military strength, or proximity to the region's geographic center to make a serious bid for leadership. Moreover, antipathy toward Egypt's peace treaty with Israel was on the wane in the Arab world, and recognition was growing that military action would not solve the Arab-Israeli dispute. Saddam Hussein's defeat in the Gulf war, during which he revived the idea of military struggle with Israel, not only diminished the stature of Egypt's chief Arab competitor, it also made the Arab-Israeli peace option more salient. Leadership in the Arab world in the 1990s, therefore, appears to center on how an Arab state can address broader Arab concerns from the "outside"—namely, vis-à-vis Israel and the West. The defeat of Saddam Hussein has enabled Egypt to assert this political role, with few detractors. Egypt's success, however, depends on whether it can actually deliver political benefits to the Arabs. If it is unable to do so, then those Arab states that are currently acquiescing to Egypt's more prominent role in shaping Arab affairs (such as in the peace process and in the Arab League) could turn against Cairo.

The Arab world of the 1990s is a much different place than that of the 1950s and 1960s, and Hosni Mubarak is much different from Gamal Abd al-Nasir. Yet what is similar about these periods is that Egypt is using the resources at its disposal to ride the political waves in the Arab world for the benefit of its national interests. Nasir did not invent pan-Arabism, but he wholly embraced it after it captured the imagination of millions of Arabs. The militancy of the period, and the Cold War rivalry, which enabled the Arabs to obtain Soviet weaponry, affected the Arabs' belief that the Arab-Israeli dispute could be solved militarily. Egypt thus relied on its military primacy in the Arab world and its charismatic president to project the image of regional leader. In the 1990s Egypt has benefited by a new pragmatism that has come to the political forefront in the Arab world, helped by the demise of the Soviet Union, which effectively ended the Arabs' military option in the Arab-Israeli dispute. The end of the Cold War, however, has elicited Arab fears that the Arab world has lost influence and protection. Egypt is telling the Arabs that because of Cairo's international stature, diplomatic experience, and military capability, it can protect and advance Arab rights. Egypt's leadership role in the 1990s cannot match that of the 1950s and 1960s. But in both periods, Egyptian officials believed that in their quest for Arab leadership, they would solve pressing domestic needs.

CHAPTER 4

DOMESTIC DETERMINANTS
OF EGYPTIAN FOREIGN POLICY

" . . . any positive outcome achieved on the foreign policy level will have its effects on internal political and
economic performance."—President Mubarak, in remarks to Egyptian legislators, April 15, 1992

Population pressures, grinding poverty among the
masses, and the dearth of meaningful employment
opportunities have traditionally led Egyptian
leaders to seek foreign assistance to alleviate these
problems. Egypt has looked to the Arab world as the
natural arena for outside help because of linguistic,
cultural, and religious affinities, even though the
general Egyptian populace has long held an ambig-
uous attitude toward the Arab world. Egyptian political activists, however, have more often than not
attached themselves to political causes that fall outside of narrow Egyptian interests, such as the Palestinian question and the conditions of Muslims
under siege. Egyptian political leaders, therefore,
must demonstrate that they are sensitive to these
concerns. Additionally, they seem to believe that
Arab states will be more inclined to come to Egypt's
economic aid if Egypt takes up Arab causes.

Thus, the old adage that domestic pressures
force a regime to look inward does not apply in
Egypt's case. In fact, just the opposite occurs. Be-

cause Egypt cannot solve its economic problems on its own, and because oppositionists within Egypt frequently seize on issues that concern the broader Arab and Muslim world, Egyptian leaders must spend much of their time in the foreign policy arena, particularly where Arab issues are involved. Increasing economic and political pressures at home are, therefore, the chief engines driving Egypt's Arab policy.

ECONOMIC DETERMINANTS

Egypt has been in a chronic economic crisis for decades. In brief, its basic problems have been the lack of arable land (96 percent of the people live on only 4 percent of the land) and a population explosion (its population of 55–60 million increased by 14 million since 1980). Since 1900, cultivated land has expanded by only 25 percent, while the population has increased by 380 percent.[1] In addition, Egypt has limited foreign exchange earnings (from oil, worker remittances, tourism, and Suez canal tolls), which are vulnerable to economic and political trends, and a bloated public sector, which has led to mismanagement and waste. Moreover, the country's extensive system of consumer subsidies, amid a system of poor tax collection, has contributed to large, unsustainable budget deficits. Most Egyptians live at subsistence levels; per capita gross domestic product for 1990 was only $473.[2]

Egyptians have generally not taken their economic frustrations to the street, believing that they can do little to improve their station in life. But on three occasions in the recent past, the security forces were called in to restore order when segments of the population reacted violently to economic issues. In January 1977 food riots broke out in Cairo following government announcements that the price of bread and other consumer goods had risen in response to International Monetary Fund (IMF) guidelines. Security forces killed scores of city dwellers, and the government quickly rescinded the price increases to avoid further disturbances. In 1986 several thousand police conscripts (who received extremely low pay) rioted in response to rumors that their length of service would be extended. More recently, hundreds of Egyptians made homeless by the October 1992 earthquake rioted in central Cairo against what they perceived as government indifference to their plight. Hundreds of people first demonstrated in front of government offices, then became unruly, throwing rocks, smashing windows, damaging shops, and burning tires. The police made scores of arrests and sealed off several streets in downtown Cairo. Some of the rioters directed their anger at President Mubarak personally.[3] These three incidents shook the stability of the Egyptian polity.

The October 1992 riot is symptomatic of the deep feelings of frustration that ordinary Egyptians are experiencing over their economic situation. Living standards have declined in recent years as price rises have outpaced wage increases. Moreover, dismal job prospects for Egyptian youth are, in part, fueling Egypt's underground Islamic extremist movement, which has fomented sectarian strife and engaged in antigovernment terrorism intermittently since the early 1980s. The most sustained period of Islamic extremist violence occurred in 1992. The government has responded forcefully to this violence by arresting large numbers of suspected Islamic extremists and imposing curfews in the most affected areas.

In response to these pressures, Cairo has become consumed with the maintenance of domestic stability. The most obvious example of this preoccupation was its hesitancy in the late 1980s to reach an agreement with the IMF, believing that the extent and pace of IMF demands for economic reform would lead to social unrest. Mubarak stated: "Economic reform has many conditions. . . . I was not able to take these steps at first because I was afraid for the citizens; I was afraid for the people."[4] After Egypt finally signed an agreement with the IMF in 1991, Mubarak declared that economic reform must be an "Egyptian reform," capable of maintaining "a balance with the international system and keeping the social balance in Egypt."[5]

In the foreign policy arena, Egypt has, in large part, pursued policies over the past several decades to aid its troubled economy at home:

> In the 1970s economic factors played a crucial role in the determination of Egypt's foreign policy objectives. By 1980, inflation was running nearly 30% a year, debts reached a total of $17 billion, and the GNP per capita was $580. Sadat's decision to visit Israel was largely motivated by economic considerations: reduction in defense expenditures (37% of the GNP in 1977), the encouragement of foreign private capital, and the need for more U.S. aid. Even before this step, Sadat's Arab policy and his forging of a Cairo-Riyadh alliance had also been predicated on expected economic gains.[6]

As a result of the Gulf war—which brought an infusion of Saudi and Gulf Arab aid and helped to cancel the $7 billion U.S. military debt, saving Egypt some $850 million in payments a year— Egypt's balance of payments situation improved.[7] However, the return of several hundred thousand

Egyptian workers from Iraq and Kuwait exacer-
bated the country's already severe unemployment
problem.

No accurate figures are available on the jobless
rate in Egypt (estimates range from 10 percent to 20
percent).[8] While official unemployment may be
lower than reported rates in other developing countries, Egypt is relatively distinctive in that approximately 85 percent of its jobless are technical school
or university graduates.[9] In addition, a large propor-
tion (perhaps 30–40 percent) of Egyptian young people are underemployed, pursuing marginal work
such as selling cigarettes on the street. In the words
of one scholar, "they form a nervous mass, anxious
for a change in Egyptian society, many waiting to be
mobilized by some political movement. They fill the
nightmares of Cairo officials."[10] Moreover, Mubarak
has stated that if he went along with the recommen-
dations of some of his economic advisors to reduce
the size of the armed forces, "these sons would have
nothing to do outside the Army and would become
unemployed. What would you do then?"[11]

Unemployment is, therefore, the most serious
economic problem facing Egypt today, and one that
is likely to grow worse in the coming years as the
government closes public-sector outlets for new en-
trants to the job market and streamlines public-
sector companies in accordance with its economic
reform program. The extent and seriousness of this
problem is not lost on Egyptian policymakers. In
fact, it seems central to their domestic and foreign
policy goals. In an interview in Egypt's most widely
read paper in early February 1992, Mubarak stated
that finding jobs for Egyptian youth is his first priority. He went on to say: "We have to create approx-

imately half a million jobs every year. . . . In seeking ways to create new jobs, we have to look for labor-intensive projects that provide jobs quickly."[12] Additionally, in his Labor Day address in 1992, Mubarak sought to assure the Egyptian people:

> Brothers and sisters, I do not believe that I have to tell you that I am aware of the difficulties every Egyptian suffers daily due to high prices, unemployment, and the problems of education and other services. . . . I am also aware that many are concerned that their children will not be able to find suitable employment opportunities. I am aware of all these hardships and am trying to do everything I can to alleviate their impact on the honest and toiling citizens.[13]

The president has also tried to explain government economic priorities to the populace. He stated on several occasions that during the 1980s Egypt had to concentrate on improving the country's deteriorating infrastructure, noting that the government spent 70 billion Egyptian pounds in this area. Now, with most major infrastructure projects completed, Egypt had to concentrate on its citizens' welfare: "Economic development requires job opportunities for every citizen and an acceptable standard of living."[14] With Egypt needing to create nearly half a million jobs per year, "we should look for labor-intensive areas in which new jobs can be found—an arduous task."[15]

The task of finding 500,000 jobs for Egyptians is indeed a daunting problem. The government policy of guaranteeing every university graduate a job in the civil service, initiated during Nasir's rule, is no longer viable because of the pressing need to cut back public-sector waste and redundancy.

The government has three realistic options to mitigate the massive unemployment problem. The first is to adhere to its new economic reform program, which has the potential to produce long-term growth and create jobs in the private sector. Closely tied to this reform program is the second option— attracting foreign investment and directing it to labor-intensive projects and ventures. The third option is to find job markets outside of Egypt for the excess work force.

The first option is the one Egypt will ultimately have to rely on to create jobs over the long term, especially since the other two choices depend, to a large extent, on the good will of friendly states operating in an uncertain political and economic climate. However, it will take many years before Egypt—if it adheres to the economic reform program—will be in a position to generate enough economic growth to meet its job demand. Recognizing this problem, international donors in 1991 pledged $400 million to create a World Bank–sponsored social fund—the purpose of which is to provide jobs to the neediest in society (chiefly through infrastructure projects such as canal cleaning) and to provide business loans to university graduates. Egypt has been criticized by economists for the slow pace at which it has tried to set up mechanisms to disburse the funds,[16] though in June 1992 Cairo announced that the social fund had reportedly allocated $150 million to university graduates to set up small-scale projects.[17] Even if these projects get under way, employment will still be below the job curve, because the labor force is growing faster than private-sector jobs are being created.

The government has to do more and cannot afford to wait until economic growth picks up. It must pursue the other two options to ease the economic and political pressures that have arisen from the jobless crisis. First, the Egyptian leadership, in conjunction with Syria, is attempting to put pressure on the GCC states to follow through on their pledge to create a special fund to aid those Arab states that came to their assistance in the Gulf crisis. If the fund materializes, Egypt is likely to be the major beneficiary. In the meantime, individual GCC states have signed bilateral agreements with Cairo to fund certain infrastructure and public-sector projects in Egypt.[18] However, investment from private businessmen from the GCC states has been small, and limited mainly to Egypt's deregulated tourist industry. Egypt has begun to remove some impediments to foreign investment to facilitate this process elsewhere,[19] but some observers believe that private-sector investors will remain reluctant to put their money into Egypt until Cairo's economic reform program shows sustained progress.

During Egypt's first experience with economic liberalization (Sadat's *infitah*, or opening), foreign investors had, in general, an unhappy experience in dealing with the legendary bottlenecks of the Egyptian bureaucracy.[20] Despite the close relations that developed between Washington and Cairo during the Sadat era, American private business investment in Egypt was disappointingly low from Cairo's perspective; the Europeans did not show much enthusiasm, either.[21] Arab investment was significant,[22] though many Arab businessmen, like their non-Arab counterparts, were frustrated by Egypt's numerous business regulations, which led them to curtail their investments.[23] Egypt has recently removed some—though by no means all—impediments to foreign investment, but outside investors are not rushing back in. So far, Arab private-sector investment in Egypt has been only a trickle,[24] and some observers believe that it is unlikely to pick up until Cairo follows through on its economic reform program. Even then, private Saudi and other Arab Gulf investors may be reluctant to sink their money into Egypt. Egyptian officials seem to believe that for political reasons, these Arab private investors may have to be prodded by their own governments to invest money into Egypt.

The third option, to create jobs for Egyptian workers, also involves the political cooperation of the Arab states. Given its population pressures, Egypt has a great need to expand its job markets outside of the country. It has traditionally looked to the Arab world for this source; this is unlikely to change, even though Egyptian officials are looking increasingly to Europe for job markets, and it may explain why Mubarak has floated the idea of a Mediterranean Club (an economic grouping of Mediterranean states). Given the growing resentment toward immigrants and foreign workers in Europe, however, Egypt is unlikely to be able to boost its modest work force there. Therefore, the Arab world will continue to be the major destination of Egyptian job seekers.

In 1980 about 9 percent of the Egyptian work force was employed in various Arab states.[25] Access to these job markets is important not only for the employment it provides, but for the billions of dollars in remittances it brings to Egypt.[26] In addition, access to these jobs plays an important social role, offering working-class Egyptians the opportunity to improve their economic standing once they return home and to create a better future for their children by providing them with housing, for example.[27]

Since the end of the Gulf war, Egypt has vigorously sought jobs for its workers in Arab countries, especially since it lost several hundred thousand jobs in Iraq and Kuwait. Total Egyptian employment in the Arab world dropped from 2.33 million in June 1990 to 1.37 million in May 1991. Four months later, however, it had risen to 2.43 million. The Arab states that took in the largest number of Egyptians during this time were Saudi Arabia and Libya. The Egyptian work force in Saudi Arabia increased from 565,000 in June 1990 to 1 million in September 1991. Unskilled workers accounted for most of the increase, probably making up for the expulsion of Yemeni workers during the Gulf crisis. In Libya the Egyptian work force grew spectacularly, from only 85,000 in June 1990 to 1 million in September 1991,[28] though most workers were probably employed only part-time. According to some Egyptian officials, by the spring of 1992 the Egyptian work force in Libya had grown to 1.5 million,[29] and the Egyptian work force in Kuwait had reached 70 percent of pre–Gulf crisis levels, or 140,000.

The Arab countries are doubtless going through a period of economic sluggishness, and the Egyptian work force in these states is unlikely to expand greatly. Nonetheless, the large number of Egyptian workers employed in various Arab states represents some 14 percent of the total Egyptian work force and is an enormous economic and political relief to the Egyptian government. But achieving this level and maintaining it takes political clout, and Egypt was able to do this only by returning to the Arab world, defending Arab causes, and courting old enemies, such as Libyan leader Muammar Qadhafi.

The interplay between Egypt's leadership role in Arab politics and the economic benefits that such a role accrues is not new. A study of the Palestinian question in Egyptian politics has noted:

> The Wafd's [Egypt's liberal-nationalist party] interest in strengthening pan-Arab ties, or at least coopting pan-Arab plans, was clearly motivated by more than a desire to wrest the leadership of the Arab bloc from Transjordan and Iraq. By the early 1940s, and with the independence of much of the Arab region, new economic realities began to attract Egypt's attention. Various segments of the Egyptian political elite, and certainly the Wafd, began to look to Arab markets as a potential outlet for their surplus products and labor force. . . . During its interwar period, moreover, large numbers of Egyptian university graduates were unable to find employment at home. Both Egypt's bureaucracy and its economic institutions failed to absorb the new graduates and Iraq became the first Arab country to employ a large contingent of Egyptian educators. Even the intellectuals' call for greater cooperation was motivated by the need to seek outlets for Egypt's expanding publishing houses and movie industries. The native Egyptian bourgeoisie, the backbone of the Wafd, was also expanding its institutions in the Arab world.[30]

POLITICAL DETERMINANTS

Many observers of the Egyptian domestic scene make the argument that the Mubarak government faces no unmanageable political challenges—the opposition is hopelessly divided and has proven to be inept in mounting any effective challenge to central authority. The boycott of the last parliamentary election, in late 1990, by four opposition parties left only the small, leftist Tagammu party as the official opposition in the People's Assembly (with six seats out of 448). Moreover, the violent Islamic extremist groups, while demonstrating a capacity to stage terrorist attacks against security forces and officials, have little support among the majority of Egyptians and have been marginalized by the regime's extensive security forces. Finally, the dire economic straits of the Egyptian people do not portend a social revolution, as was the case in Algeria, because the Egyptian masses have been poor for countless centuries, do not believe they can move out of their station in life, and never went through a period of rising expectations that were dashed by a sharp economic decline.

This picture, while partly accurate, ignores the inherent weaknesses of the Egyptian political system and political and social trends in present-day Egypt. For one, government legitimacy in Egypt since Nasir's time was in part a result of a social contract between the state and the people. The government promised its citizens that in exchange for political support, it would take care of their education, health, and work needs. Education was free through the university level, and every university graduate was promised a job in the civil service. This system allowed the rural middle class and the urban lower-middle class the opportunity to advance their status in society.[31] The system worked for a time, but severe population pressures and a deteriorating economy, made worse by large military expenditures, made the social contract untenable as the decades progressed. In its place, Islamic associations—which the Sadat regime allowed to operate as a bulwark against leftists—began to create institutions such as workshops for unemployed youth, health clinics, and day-care centers. The Muslim Brotherhood has run many of these institutions, thus attracting a growing number of Egyptians to its ranks.

Under the Mubarak government, the Muslim Brotherhood has functioned in a semilegal status. Cairo has refused the Brotherhood's repeated requests to obtain full rights as a political party, but has allowed it to operate openly and take part in parliamentary elections in alliance with other opposition parties. The Brotherhood, therefore, is pursuing a two-track policy. On the one hand it is trying to create a state within a state. Through its extensive social welfare institutions, it is demonstrating to the Egyptian people that the secular state is increasingly irrelevant to their daily lives. This was most evident in the immediate aftermath of the 1992 earthquake, when the Brotherhood rushed to set up relief tents for the victims, preempting the government's own relief initiatives.[32] The Brothers believe that over time, enough Egyptians will drift to their side so that the secular state will lose any remaining legitimacy it has. On the other hand, in the short run, they are attempting to increase their support and influence by making a mark on the political landscape, such as by participating in elections (in 1984 and 1987) and pressuring the government to impose the *sharia* on society. The Egyptian constitution specifies the *sharia* as a major source of Egyptian law, but not the only source.

Cairo tolerates the Brotherhood and its activities for several reasons. Mubarak has staked his legitimacy on the notion that he has brought a certain level of democracy to Egypt. As long as the Brotherhood renounces violence, the government would lose some of that legitimacy if it denied the largest Islamic movement in Egypt a role in the nation's polity. In addition, the Brotherhood serves as a bulwark against more extreme Islamic movements, such as the violence-prone Jihad or Gama'at, which have periodically assassinated regime figures and fomented sectarian strife for the past decade.[33] Furthermore, as a practical matter, the social welfare institutions created by the Brotherhood relieve the regime of some financial burdens since the government cannot maintain the Nasirite social contract at the level society demands. Finally, and perhaps more importantly, tolerating the Brotherhood allows the government to ride the ideological waves in the Arab world. Secular nationalism and socialism are widely perceived to be failures in the Arab world, and some form of political Islam is on the rise. Tolerating the Brotherhood allows Cairo to demonstrate that it is sensitive to these trends. The government has also acted in a more "Islamic" way in recent years (and Mubarak is publicly acting in a way that connotes devotion to Islamic principles). It has encouraged more religious programs to appear on television, allowed the judiciary to issue sentences against so-called blasphemous writers,[34] and even suggested that it favors more Islamic punishments (one state judge suggested in February 1992 that drug dealers be hanged publicly in the place where they sold narcotics).[35]

These policies suggest that Mubarak is pursuing a strategy of managing the Egyptian political landscape largely by preempting the opposition. Some observers may believe that, given the weak state of the opposition, such a policy is unnecessary. But that view disregards the historical role of the intelligentsia, derived from the middle class, in Egyptian politics.

The Egyptian middle class has developed somewhat differently from its counterparts in other

Third World states, but its experience is not unique, given the socialist experiments of many states in the post–World War II era. The entrepreneurial section of the middle class in Egypt tended to be in the hands of minorities, such as Greeks, Jews, Armenians, Syrians, and Lebanese. Nasir's socialist policies nationalized most of their businesses and contributed to the emigration of these groups. The Egyptian Muslim middle class never had the opportunity to develop into a large commercial middle class in their place because of the nationalization policies and the expansion of civil service jobs, which worked to co-opt the middle class into the government. The government guarantee that every university graduate would have a place in the civil service facilitated this process. Additionally, in the 1960s, civil service wages grew at a rate in excess of the national wage bill.[36] By 1980 public-sector workers (including white-collar civil servants and state industrial workers, but excluding teachers and armed forces personnel) accounted for one-third of the Egyptian work force (3.2 million out of 10 million).[37]

The combination of falling real wages in the 1980s and a more tolerant political system led the better-educated segment of the middle class— the intelligentsia—to criticize the government more openly. Broadly defined, the intelligentsia in Egypt encompasses academics, journalists, university students, technocrats, Western-educated businessmen, and middle- and high-ranking civil servants. It is among these segments of society that the opposition draws its support. The Egyptian intelligentsia has always played a political role far greater than its numbers indicate. For one, it was instrumental in the development of the Arab cultural renaissance, and its writers achieved widespread admiration in the Arab world. It also played an important role in the development of political parties. And today, with adult illiteracy in Egypt still at very high levels (perhaps 40 percent), the intelligentsia remains the pulse of the ideological and political trends in the country. One scholar has noted:

> Ever since the French Expedition to Egypt, intellectuals have acted as the guardians of Egypt's soul. At first religious in orientation, such as al-Azhar Shaikhs who defied the French, Egypt's intellectuals maintained their unparalleled position of national direction and leadership until the modern period. In later years, secular and religious, modern and traditionalist intellectuals vied with each other for the role of guardian of the Egyptian heritage. Egyptian intellectuals, whether included or excluded from participation in government, continued to define and debate national issues.[38]

It must be remembered that President Sadat had alienated the intelligentsia in the months preceding his assassination. For instance, in September 1981—one month before he was killed—his security forces rounded up some 1,600 moderate oppositionists and intellectuals; this action severely eroded Sadat's already weak public support. Such incidents undoubtedly had a profound effect on Mubarak, who was then vice president. As president, Mubarak has often stated that democracy[39] is Egypt's "safety valve."

The opposition parties also have an influence greater than their numbers indicate because they maintain party newspapers that are widely read by the intelligentsia. Moreover, under Mubarak's regime, these party newspapers have been relatively free to voice their opposition to government policies. Mubarak is, however, sensitive to their criticism. In his 1992 Labor Day address, he stated: "I appeal to the Egyptian press—both the national and party press—to heed God and examine carefully what they publish to safeguard the country's reputation and interests and to avoid exaggerations and generalizations that damage Egypt's image and society."[40] He has also said: "I follow up writers' articles, and sometimes I read something improper, and tell the writer that it is not right."[41]

What influence does the intelligentsia, both the secular and the religious, have on Egyptian foreign policy formulation? For one, the growth of Islamic consciousness and the strength of the Muslim Brotherhood force the regime to make numerous public pronouncements on Islamic and Palestinian issues. In late October 1991 a few hundred Muslim fundamentalist students at Cairo University protested against the upcoming Madrid peace conference, denouncing the United States and Israel.[42] The Muslim Brotherhood also denounced the conference.[43] Mubarak then went to Cairo University in early November and told the students and faculty:

> We shall not budge an inch on the Jerusalem issue. You probably know that I gave an interview to the *New York Times* a week before the conference. The interviewer came here and held the interview to publish it on the day of the conference. He asked me about Jerusalem. I sent a message to the Israeli prime minister once and told him to please stop talking about Jerusalem because it is a very sensitive issue since it deals with religion. I told them that it was an issue just as sensitive to the Arabs, the Muslims, and the Christians as it was to them. . . . We still uphold the Jerusalem issue and no one has disregarded it. Jerusalem is the third Holy Mosque and no one can ever disregard it.[44]

Seven months later, Mubarak again weighed in on the issue of Jerusalem, in his toughest speech yet. Read by Foreign Minister Musa at the Arab League headquarters in Cairo on Jerusalem Day, June 6, 1992, Mubarak's speech stated in part:

> Continued Israeli occupation of Arab and Palestinian land in the West Bank and Gaza, regardless of its duration or nature, cannot create rights or establish legitimacy. It is based on claims that are falsely attributed to a religion, illusions that distort history, and excuses for expansionist dreams. . . . What applies to the occupied Palestinian territories also applies, in the same manner, degree, and logic, to the Arab city of Jerusalem, which is an integral part of those territories.[45]

These speeches were a reflection of a nuanced shift in Egyptian official statements since 1991, toward a sharper criticism of Israeli policies under Yitzhak Shamir. On the peace process, Foreign Minister Musa has emphasized that Egypt is not a neutral party to the Arab-Israeli negotiations, but part of the Arab side.[46] In his speech at the Madrid peace conference in early November 1991, after the Arab foreign ministers and Israeli Prime Minister Shamir exchanged inflammatory accusations, Musa remarked: "We have listened to some passionate speeches which manifest how a change in attitudes is badly needed. I address Israel mainly."[47] Furthermore, Musa has constantly reiterated that Israel must accept the land-for-peace principle and the Palestinian people's right to self-determination.[48] He has also stated that it is inconceivable that a comprehensive peace will be achieved when "building Israeli settlements continues, when the Palestinian people's right to self-determination continues to be denied, and when stubbornness and stalemate continue as the norm regarding the Jerusalem issue."[49]

Egyptian officials no doubt have an eye to the broader Arab world when issuing such statements, but these comments also deflect public criticism at home from opposition circles that the government is not doing enough to protect and advance Muslim and Palestinian rights.

Cairo has pursued policies in other areas to stem the concerns of the intelligentsia at home. In particular, reports about the suffering of the Iraqi people at the end of the Gulf war produced guilt feelings among Egyptian intellectuals who supported the war against Baghdad. In response, Egyptian officials have expressed sympathy with the plight of the Iraqis, and Egypt was the first of the anti-Saddam Arab coalition states to call for the lifting of economic sanctions against Iraq in the summer of 1991.[50]

In addition, in early 1992 a strong sentiment emerged among Egyptian intellectuals that the United States and the other Western powers were out to punish Iraq and Libya while ignoring Israeli violations of human rights and other international norms. One Egyptian correspondent for *Al-Ahram* stated: "From our perspective this new world order translates into a combination of benign neglect for Arabs, punctuated with selective punishment as we see with Iraq and Libya. . . . It is a vengeful new order."[51] Other Egyptian writers attributed the Western policies against Iraq and Libya to deepseated racial and cultural prejudices against Arabs and Muslims.[52]

The belief that the United States and the other Western powers would ride roughshod over the Arabs in the absence of the Soviet Union was probably partly responsible for Egypt's active role in trying to defuse the reemergence of the Pan Am 103 controversy between Libya and the Security Council in the spring of 1992. Egypt tried to use the Arab League to undertake mediation efforts in an effort to show that Egypt did its utmost to protect the Arab homeland. A Cairo radio commentary pointed out that "President Mubarak's efforts gave all the parties time to think and reconsider. More importantly, these efforts have succeeded—through the Arab League—in curbing as far as possible the severity of the sanctions against Libya. We must admit that these efforts have almost ruled out any military action against Libya."[53] Egyptian newspapers, both progovernment and opposition, castigated Washington for being unduly harsh on Libya, and a delegation of Egypt's opposition parties that traveled to Libya in late May 1992 stated that "this malicious campaign is not only directed against the Great Jamhariyah [Libya] but against the entire Arab and Islamic world."[54]

Egypt's dire economic troubles and its somewhat fragile political system have, therefore, moved the government to play a leading role in Arab affairs. Active engagement in Arab affairs helps to ensure badly needed jobs for Egyptian workers in various Arab states and helps to lure Arab investment for labor-intensive ventures at home. Several political measures—coordination with the Arab parties to the peace process; demonstrations of sympathy with the Palestinian, Libyan, and Iraqi peoples; and outspokenness in regard to the Jerusalem issue—work to mitigate the criticism of Islamists and other oppositionists that the Mubarak government is too close to the United States and is not doing enough to protect and advance Arab and Muslim interests. As Egypt continues on its difficult path of economic reform—leading the government to spend more time managing stability—we can expect it to play an even more active role in Arab affairs to defuse domestic tensions.

CHAPTER 5

IMPLICATIONS FOR U.S. POLICY

The close relations between the United States and Egypt since the late 1970s, and the political and military cooperation between the two countries during Desert Shield and Desert Storm in 1990–1991, may give the impression that the U.S.-Egyptian relationship is, for the most part, solid and relatively free of divisiveness. Bolstering this notion is the fact that Egypt is the second largest U.S. aid recipient—receiving $2.3 billion annually in military and economic assistance. Egypt has cooperated with the United States on various incarnations of the peace process since the Camp David accords, and Washington has considered Egypt a "strategic asset" in the region. Yet this assessment belies inherent problems in the relationship. Moreover, in 1992 Cairo and Washington found themselves pursuing different policies toward Libya and Iraq. As the 1990s progress, Egypt's delicate balancing act between its U.S. and Arab interests is likely to tilt more heavily toward the latter because of its problems at home and the economic and political benefits it accrues from pursuing an Arab leadership role.

Placing U.S.-Egyptian relations in a broad perspective, one scholar has noted: "One need not look back very far to be reminded of how unusual it is for

Cairo and Washington to be on good terms. From the mid-1950s through the early 1970s, against a backdrop of regional instability and regional crises, the United States and Egypt typically found themselves at odds."[1] Even during the 1980s—after the signing of the Camp David accords—relations between Cairo and Washington went through some difficult periods, such as during the Israeli invasion of Lebanon in 1982 and the *Achille Lauro* affair in 1985.[2]

Close U.S.-Egyptian relations developed during the Sadat era, after the October 1973 war. Sadat's embrace of the United States was a reflection of his personal mistrust of the Soviet Union, his belief that the United States would help solve Egypt's massive economic problems, and his belief that only the United States could influence Israeli policies and ensure the return of captured territory.[3] By the late 1970s Sadat had become strongly anti-Soviet. He "cautioned the United States against underestimating the Soviet threat and pointed out that U.S. influence in the region was on the wane."[4] In addition, Sadat was eager to forge close strategic links between the two countries. He tried to sell the notion that Egypt could become an asset for Western strategy in the region, and the United States and Egypt collaborated in military training and maneuvers.[5]

Placing Egypt squarely in the American camp and signing the Camp David accords was Sadat's response to the needs of Egypt's national interests. In doing so, however, he alienated much of the Arab world, even his conservative backers in the Gulf region, such as Saudi Arabia. Sadat responded to the subsequent Arab boycott of Egypt with contempt, castigating his Arab detractors as "ignorant dwarfs." Cairo's official media put out the line that Egypt had done more than its share for the Arab-Israeli cause, and that pressing economic needs necessitated securing a peace treaty with Israel.[6] Accompanying these explanations was the development of an "Egypt-first" ideology, which downplayed Egypt's Arab identity and stressed its Nile/Mediterranean roots. Arab political and diplomatic ostracism of Egypt, along with the cutoff of Arab aid, made Egypt increasingly dependent on the United States. One scholar has noted that Arab governments, "in imposing economic sanctions on Egypt, thought that Egypt could not do without their aid. This did not prove to be the case."[7] U.S. economic and military aid cushioned the impact of the Arab boycott, but U.S. assistance did not lead to the turnaround of the Egyptian economy that Sadat had hoped for.

The continuation of Egypt's economic crisis and the gradual return of Egyptian public opinion in favor of involvement in Arab affairs[8] motivated Cairo to improve ties with the Arab world. Moreover, Egypt's dependence on the United States had hurt its nonaligned image and provided the leftist and Islamist opposition with an issue to exploit. Mubarak, therefore, embarked on a diplomatic program to bring a balance to Egyptian foreign policy. By 1990 Egypt had reestablished relations with the Arab world while keeping its peace treaty with Israel intact. Cairo also restored relations with the Soviet Union, reaffirmed its position in the nonaligned movement, and hosted a meeting of the Socialist International, while maintaining close ties to the United States.

The Gulf crisis, as mentioned earlier, allowed Mubarak the opportunity to exercise leadership in Arab affairs, or at least among those Arab states that opposed the Iraqi invasion of Kuwait. Egypt's close political and military cooperation with the United States during the crisis, however, elicited a great deal of controversy in certain Arab circles and among oppositionists within Egypt itself. Mubarak nonetheless pursued an unwavering policy against Saddam Hussein and lent military support and troops to oust Iraqi forces from Kuwait. However, the Egyptian president remained sensitive to charges that he was acting at the behest of Washington. He frequently stated that Egypt supported the liberation of Kuwait out of its "pan-Arab responsibilities." Similar concerns arose during the resurfacing of the Pan Am 103 controversy in the spring of 1992. After criticizing the United States and the Security Council for not letting diplomacy run its course, Egypt nonetheless agreed to abide by Security Council sanctions against Libya. But Mubarak told a group of journalists in June 1992 that "Egypt is not being used politically or militarily. It is a leader and makes its own decisions."[9]

Disparate Egyptian opposition parties are divided on a host of issues, but opposition to U.S. policies is what often brings them together. For example, a prominent Nasirist stated in mid-1992 that the Muslim Brotherhood had moved closer to the leftist, Arab nationalist Nasirist position on two main issues, one of which is: "America is the principal enemy of the nation."[10]

The Gulf war and the end of the Cold War increased the level of anti-Americanism in certain Egyptian circles. While many of Egypt's oppositionists opposed the Iraqi invasion of Kuwait, they also opposed the stationing of non-Muslim troops in Saudi Arabia during Desert Shield and Western and Arab coalition military efforts to oust Iraq from Kuwait. Moreover, Islamists interpreted the air strikes against Iraq during Desert Storm as a way for the West to punish Iraq for daring to stand up to the United States and Israel. They also saw the attacks on Iraq's military installations and infrastructure as a way to weaken the Arabs' collective military strength to the benefit of the West and Israel. The Soviets' lack of support for Saddam Hussein in the Gulf crisis demonstrated to Egypt's leftists how the end of the Cold War worked to their disadvantage. The demise of the Soviet Union shortly thereafter spelled danger for Islamists and leftists, who believed that it gave the United States an opportunity to dictate terms to the Arab world with impunity.

In addition to the perception that the Arabs and Muslims have lost strategic ground in the post–Cold War world, a new twist to the old argument about "Western cultural imperialism" developed in the region—particularly among Islamists. Since the 1980s, Islamists have eagerly read books and articles about Western bias against Arabs and Muslims. The popularity of such studies has contributed to the notion that cultural attitudes, more than political or economic interests, determine U.S. policy in the region. Many Islamists believe that the Bush administration's strong stand against Yitzhak Shamir's settlement policies debunked the view, widely held in the Arab world, that U.S. foreign policy is controlled by "Zionist interests." What instead is driving U.S. policy in the region, they argue, is a deep-seated Western prejudice toward Arabs and Muslims.[11]

Reflective of these sentiments, Egyptians were stirred by reports of Serbian attacks on the Muslims of Bosnia in 1992. One Cairo newspaper noted: "Syndicates of engineers, lawyers, pharmacists, and the opposition Islamic-oriented Socialist Labor Party are all taking part in the campaign [to protest the attacks on Bosnian Muslims], arousing religious feelings and warning of the 'Western offensive' against Islam."[12] Domestic sentiments may have prompted Egypt to send troops to join UN peace-keeping forces in Bosnia. In addition, Cairo's establishment *Al-Akhbar* editorialized that if the "major countries are still content to be spectators, the Islamic countries can help the Muslim people of Bosnia-Hercegovina effectively by organizing secret operations to smuggle whatever weapons they can send."[13]

The Egyptian government, therefore, has a fundamental political interest in extricating itself from the perception that it is dependent on the United States. And while Egypt and the United States will probably see eye to eye on certain political or strategic issues in the coming years, Egypt will also be inclined to pursue policies that will be at variance with U.S. policy and interests. The close U.S.-Egyptian collaboration that occurred in the Gulf crisis may, in fact, be more the exception than the rule.

Egypt took a strong and decisive stand in the Gulf crisis for its own strategic reasons. Cairo saw the Iraqi invasion of Kuwait as a direct threat to its leadership bid in the Arab world and to the military balance of power in the region, and as a threat to its financial benefactors in the Gulf region, particularly Saudi Arabia.[14] Although Mubarak may have believed that the United States would not let the Iraqi occupation of Kuwait stand—and reasoned that it would be advantageous for Egypt to be on the winning side—the considerations mentioned above were probably the predominant factors in his decision.

Since the end of the Gulf war, U.S. and Egyptian policies in the region have not been in congruence over certain issues; chief among them has been Libya. The Egyptians have no great love for Libyan leader Qadhafi, who was once a bitter enemy of the Sadat and Mubarak governments. Since the late 1980s, however, Egyptian officials have courted Qadhafi in the hope that Libya would open up its doors to Egyptian workers, technical expertise, and products, and that Libya would play a less meddlesome role in inter-Arab politics. Cairo believes its rapprochement with Libya has produced tangible results, including increased trade (by mid-1992 Egyptian exports to Libya were running at $25 million a month, up from minuscule amounts in the mid-1980s);[15] acceptance of large numbers of Egyptian workers; and political cooperation, such as Qadhafi's opposition to Iraq's invasion of Kuwait and his relative acquiescence on the peace process orchestrated by the United States in the autumn of 1991. Problems do occasionally scar the rapprochement, such as reports of ill treatment meted out to Egyptian workers in Libya in early 1992, and Egyptian anger at the Libyan press for criticizing Egypt in mid-1992 and for mocking the concept of Arab solidarity. Nonetheless, Egypt believes it has a vested interest in keeping relations with Libya on track.

As mentioned earlier, Egypt and the United States found themselves at odds over the resurfacing of the Pan Am 103 controversy in late 1991 and early 1992. Cairo repeatedly protested that the Security Council was unfairly ganging up on Libya. In November 1991 Egypt warned President Bush that any military action against Libya would endanger "security and stability" in the region.[16] The Egyptian government press in March and April 1992 castigated Washington for not allowing Arab League diplomacy the time to work out an agreement between the Security Council and Libya and rushing through a sanctions bill.[17] In the end, Egypt announced that it would adhere to the sanctions because it was committed to abide by "international legitimacy," but Cairo's unhappiness was evident. Sensing they had a public relations problem on their hands, Egyptian officials and government media stressed that Mubarak had done all he could do to water down the sanctions.

In a similar vein, Cairo voiced its disapproval over reports in early 1992 that the United States was contemplating a military strike against Iraq because of Baghdad's refusal to comply with Security Council resolutions. Mubarak said that he opposed the use of force against Iraq.[18] That same month, *Al-Ahram* charged that a "new fever" was gripping the United States, "a fever to impose U.S. hegemony worldwide now that it is the one and only power in the new world order."[19]

Additionally, Cairo's role in the peace process has not always been accommodating to the United States and Israel, despite the claims of Egypt's critics. In a press conference shortly before the Madrid peace conference began, Foreign Minister Musa emphasized that Egypt is not a neutral party to the Arab-Israeli peace talks but "an Arab party."[20] Although Cairo has had differences with Damascus over Syria's failure to attend the multilateral peace talks and other issues in the peace process,[21] Egyptian officials have stated that there is "logic" to Syria's desire to boycott the multilateral talks.[22] Moreover, Musa has said:

> . . . it is unreasonable to consider any . . . cooperation in the region while Arab territories are under repressive Israeli occupation; while the Palestinian people are denied their right to self-determination; and while Israel maintains its policy of settlement in the occupied Arab territories, change and annexation of holy Jerusalem, and coercion, imprisonment, and deportation. Any progress on the multilateral negotiations would depend on achievement of tangible and fundamental progress in the bilateral negotiations."[23]

Egypt has played an important behind-the-scenes role in bringing the Arab parties to the Arab-Israeli dispute to the negotiating table, and has taken part in advising them with regard to their negotiating tactics vis-à-vis Israel. Mubarak's invitation to Israeli Prime Minister Rabin in July 1992 to visit Cairo, shortly after the Israeli Labor leader came to power, was in part an effort to energize the peace process after months of only minimal progress. At his press conference with Rabin in Cairo, Mubarak stated that "we made a big effort before the Madrid peace conference, during the Madrid peace conference, and still after the Madrid conference. We are doing the maximum efforts so as to persuade all the parties, the Arab parties, to go through [with] the peace negotiations, because we consider this vital for the whole area."[24]

Egypt is taking an active part in the peace process primarily because it considers the unresolved Palestinian problem a source of instability in the region and to demonstrate Egypt's importance to both the Arab world and the broader international community. Foreign Minister Musa told the Lebanese newspaper *Al-Anwar* that Egyptian officials "understand the situation in the region very well. We have dealt with it in various ways for the past 40 or 50 years. Our dialogue with the United States, Europe, and the international community is broad and characterized by a clarity and frankness that serves Arab interests."[25] But Egypt is also placing as much, and perhaps, more emphasis on sticking to an Arab consensus and achieving Arab political solidarity. Musa has remarked that "all of us, especially Egypt, are working to realize Arab solidarity and to set Arab action on the correct path to realize Arab objectives. . . . Egypt will not go back on that." He went on to say that Arab solidarity is the major and most important weapon bolstering the Arab stand in the peace process and emphasized that there is "comprehensive Egyptian-Arab coordination on this."[26]

Having retrieved all of its territory from Israel, persuaded the Arab League to return its headquarters to Cairo, and assumed a leadership role in the Arab world, Egypt probably believes it has little to gain, and much to lose, if it goes out on a limb in the peace process or drifts too far from core Arab demands. Moreover, Mubarak remains a cautious player, and is not prone to Sadat's grandiose gestures.[27] A prominent Egyptian columnist has written that "Egypt could be a facilitator and a trusted intermediary [between Israel and the Arabs] but it will not alienate anybody if it cannot please every-body."[28] Thus, there are limits on how far Egypt will go in trying to bridge the gap between the Arab and Israeli sides.

The advent of the Rabin government in Israel in July 1992 initially heightened Syrian concerns that the Golan Heights issue would be relegated to the back burner in the peace process deliberations, be-cause Rabin reportedly favored dealing with the Palestinian autonomy issue first.[29] The Syrian me-dia reminded its Arab peace partners that the peace process must be "comprehensive" and involve the withdrawal from all occupied territory. To allay Syrian concerns, Egyptian officials have spoken out publicly on the need for "full Israeli withdrawal from the Golan Heights"[30] and for a unified Arab position on the peace process.[31]

From Egypt's perspective, keeping Syria in the peace process is a top priority. A spurned Syria would work to scuttle the entire process, endanger the new Egyptian-Syrian political and economic re-lationship, give a boost to Palestinian radicals who remain opposed to the peace process, and ruin Egypt's leadership bid in the Arab world. Mubarak reportedly has told Rabin that Syria might under-mine the peace process if it is pushed into a corner.[32] Egypt, therefore, will pursue policies in the peace process to keep the momentum going, but will not alienate any of its Arab partners. This overriding concern to work toward Arab harmony in the peace process may run into problems with future U.S. initiatives designed to break logjams in the process.

Egyptian officials are also placing more em-phasis on their Arab relations to lessen Egypt's de-pendence on the United States for their own ideological reasons. Although most senior Egyptian officials with whom U.S. policymakers come in contact seem Western-oriented and tend to be favorably disposed to the United States, this "Westernism" is not generally deep-seated. Senior Egyptian officials, for the most part, came to political maturity during the Nasir period, when anti-Westernism was the predominant ideology in Egypt and other Arab states. Although many of these officials were uncomfortable with Egypt's close ties to the Soviet Union in the late Nasir period and do not have fond memories of the Soviet officials they dealt with,[33] they are not inherently pro-West or pro-American.[34] An example of this "latent" anti-Westernism was a dispute that arose in July 1992 over the UN response to the Bosnian crisis between the secretary-general of the United Nations, Boutros Boutros-Ghali, and Britain's representative to the Security Council, Sir David Hannay. Boutros-Ghali was reportedly irked that the British got the Security Council to adopt a British-devised peacekeeping plan without consulting him. Moreover, he cited several concerns, including the question of who will pay for the operation; how an effort in southern Europe can be justified while the tragedy in Somalia is ignored; and why a decision involving UN forces was made in London, with no UN officials present.[35]

William Quandt has summarized Egypt's resentment of a dependency relationship with the United States as follows:

> Egypt . . . is a country with broad regional ambitions and severe economic difficulties. Thus the need for outside support is especially great, but so is the resentment when its freedom for maneuver is constrained by strings tied to aid. With a population above 50 million, and a recent history as the undisputed leader of the

Arab world, Egypt cannot be classified as just one more poor, dependent third world country. . . . Egyptians are extremely proud of their country, very nationalistic, and suspicious that foreigners offering help are doing so for non-Egyptian reasons. Because of these special circumstances, Cairo's relations with outsiders will always be somewhat problematic. Independence is a cherished ideal and a pillar of any regime's legitimacy, but once Egypt turns to a major power for arms and economic assistance, it begins to slip away from nonalignment. Some price is always paid to the benefactor.[36]

Cairo may believe it has greater opportunity today to break away from this dependency relationship because it is not as economically dependent on the United States as it was a few years ago. Egypt entered the 1980s facing two harsh economic realities: the cutoff of Arab aid and a deteriorated infrastructure. U.S. assistance, despite all of the controversy associated with it,[37] helped to address these problems. The breakdown of the annual $2.3 billion U.S. economic assistance to Egypt has been as follows: $1.3 billion in military aid, chiefly for purchases of U.S. military hardware; $500 million in infrastructure and social-sector development; $115 million in cash subventions to the Egyptian government; and the remainder in concessional wheat sales and the financing of specific imports. By the beginning of the 1990s, Egypt had made great strides in waste-water programs, power-generating plants, and telecommunications.[38] Mubarak acknowledged to the Egyptian people that Egypt had to concentrate on infrastructure in the 1980s because "infrastructure is the basis for development."[39]

By the early 1990s Egypt's economic problems and priorities had changed. The Gulf war had brought about an infusion of Arab aid and the can-

cellation of Egypt's military debt to the United
States, improving Egypt's balance of payments.
Egypt, after several years of protracted negotiations, had finally signed an agreement with the IMF
in the spring of 1991, which led to a Paris Club debt
rescheduling shortly thereafter. Most major infrastructure projects had been completed, but social
problems, such as unemployment and underem-
ployment, had grown worse.[40] Moreover, Cairo's economic reform program, which called for the
reduction of consumer subsidies and thus higher
prices for certain commodities, led to increased
hardships for the Egyptian people.

Cairo and Washington signed an agreement in
1992 that would facilitate U.S. private-sector investment in Egypt,[41] but U.S. businessmen are likely to
remain hesitant, remembering the generally unhappy experiences they had under Sadat's economic
open-door policy. Foreign investment in Egypt,
therefore, is likely to remain the purview of Egypt's
Arab friends.[42] Egypt will continue to seek Arab
investment on a government-to-government basis,
will urge Arab governments to encourage their private businessmen to invest in Egypt, and will seek to
increase exports to Arab countries as a way of gener-
ating economic growth and employment.[43]

Additionally, the cancellation of the $7 billion
U.S. military debt in late 1990 has facilitated the
lessening of Egypt's economic links to the United
States. The debt issue had been an albatross around
Egypt's neck, with Egyptian officials in the uncomfortable position of periodically having to ask U.S.
policymakers for debt forgiveness.[44] The cancellation of the debt not only saved Egypt costly monthly
debt payments, but also liberated Egypt a notch

from a dependency relationship Cairo had always found distasteful. If "some price is always paid to the benefactor"[45] in a dependency relationship, then the removal of the U.S. debt may have allowed Cairo to believe it could pursue a more independent foreign policy in the region without paying a heavy price in return.

The end of the Cold War has brought another variable into the U.S.-Egyptian relationship. Sadat's desire to cast Egypt as an ally of the West in the Cold War struggle boosted Egypt's reputation in Washington and was another factor (besides keeping the peace with Israel) that helped to convince various U.S. administrations and congressmen that Egypt was worthy of some $2.3 billion annually in foreign assistance. At first glance, the end of the Cold War would seem to diminish the notion that Egypt is a strategic asset of the United States, and support the argument that Washington need not spend such large amounts on Egypt. However, Egypt demonstrated in the Gulf War—which was the first post–Cold War crisis—that it is still a strategic asset, even though it participated in that conflict for its own reasons. Thus, U.S. policymakers will probably continue to see Egypt partly in strategic terms for some time to come, given Egypt's proximity to the Gulf and U.S. strategic interests in protecting the unhindered flow of oil from that region. Additionally, as the United States grapples with the phenomenon of "political Islam" in the Arab world, Egyptian officials will probably make a compelling case to U.S. policymakers and congressmen that bolstering their economy and preventing "extremists" from exploiting the economic situation will require a continuation of U.S. aid levels. The idea of an unstable

Egypt—with its large population, proximity to Israel and Saudi Arabia, and traditional role as an intellectual center of the Arab world—would be worrisome to U.S. policymakers, to say the least. Against this backdrop, however, is the notion that the United States is headed for a period where foreign aid will increasingly become a controversial issue, given needs at home. Should Washington reduce aid to Cairo, Egypt's dependency relationship with the United States would diminish correspondingly, allowing Cairo to believe it has more room to maneuver in regional politics.

CONCLUSION

Since the late 1970s, the U.S.-Egyptian relationship has worked remarkably well and has weathered several storms. From the American perspective, U.S. political, economic, and military support to Egypt has helped to ensure that state's stability, and has lessened the possibility of a general Arab-Israeli war. There has also been an underlying assumption that, because of close bilateral ties, Cairo should cooperate with Washington in the advancement of U.S. policy goals in the region.

This assumption needs to be reassessed in light of Egypt's leadership bid in the Arab world. Close U.S.-Egyptian relations developed at a time when Egypt was "on the outs" with its Arab neighbors; had broken ties with the Soviet Union; and therefore effectively had lost its traditional economic, military, and political benefactors. Sadat's assumption that Egypt could get by without the Arab world soon proved to be untenable, not only because economic and political pressures within Egyptian society eventually militated against it, but also because Egyptian officials believed that Cairo had a historic (some would say paternalistic) role to lead the Arab world, a role that would bring to Egypt economic and political benefits. But in order to play this role, Egypt must demonstrate that it is not aiding the advancement of U.S. policy in the region. Mubarak has tried to emphasize that Egypt "is a leader and makes its own decisions."[46]

In the coming years Egypt will still value its close ties to the United States, not only to maintain present levels of economic and military aid, but to demonstrate its importance to the Arabs. With only one superpower now in existence, Cairo is pushing the idea that the Arabs need a country like Egypt (with its close U.S. ties) to convey Arab concerns and influence Washington's actions. However, there are likely to be more areas of friction in the U.S.-Egyptian relationship than there have been in the past as Egypt works to protect its more prominent role in Arab affairs. Egypt is likely to support general Arab positions on such issues as the Arab-Israeli peace process and the territorial integrity of the "Arab homeland," and will not try to influence Arab states to move behind U.S. policy in the region if "Arab rights," as broadly defined by the mood on the street or by shifting political winds, appear to be in jeopardy. The close U.S.-Egyptian relationship is, therefore, headed for a cooling period, but it need not turn cold as long as both sides understand that they have different interests and goals in the region.

NOTES

CHAPTER 2

1. Yezid Sayigh, "The Gulf Crisis: Why the Arab Regional Order Failed," *International Affairs*, vol. 67, no. 3 (1991), p. 488.
2. Many scholars make the point that modern-day power struggles between Egypt, Iraq, and Syria are a variation of the struggles between Baghdad, Damascus, and Cairo in early Islamic times. Damascus and Baghdad, for example, often cite the fact that their cities were the capitals of the Umayyad and Abbasid Islamic empires, respectively. Other scholars go back even further, pointing to the struggle for power between the ancient Egyptians and the Babylonians.
3. The Hashemites were an Arab dynasty from the Hejaz region of the Arabian peninsula who traced their descendants to the prophet Muhammad. Under the Ottomans they secured the prestigious title of guardians of the Muslim holy cities of Mecca and Medina. During the First World War the Hashemites led the British-backed Arab Revolt. Both the British and the French dashed their dreams of governing an independent Arab kingdom after the war. The British, however, installed Hashemite leaders as nominal rulers of their mandates in Iraq and Transjordan in the early 1920s. The Hashemites ruled Iraq until their violent overthrow in the revolution of 1958; they have had better luck in Jordan, where King Hussein has reigned since the early 1950s.
4. Alan Taylor, *The Arab Balance of Power* (Syracuse, N.Y.: Syracuse University Press, 1982), pp. 24–25.
5. Ibid., p. 35.
6. Malcolm H. Kerr, *The Arab Cold War: Gamal Abd al-Nasir and His Rivals, 1958–1970*, 3rd ed. (London: Oxford University Press, 1971), pp. 30–54.
7. Taylor, *The Arab Balance of Power*, p. 52.

8. Joseph Lorenz, *Egypt and the Arabs* (Boulder, Colo.: Westview Press, 1990), pp. 52–54; and Fouad Ajami, "Between Cairo and Damascus: The Arab World and the New Stalemate," *Foreign Affairs*, vol. 54, no. 3 (Spring 1976), pp. 444–445.

9. London's *Sawt al-Kuwait*, February 22, 1992, as reported in Foreign Broadcast Information Service–Near East South Asia (FBIS-NES), February 28, 1992.

10. For the full text of the Damascus Declaration states' communiqué from Qatar, see Manama WAKH, September 11, 1992, as reported in FBIS-NES, September 11, 1992.

11. See Youssef Ibrahim, "Gulf Nations Said to Be Committed to U.S. Alliance," *New York Times*, October 25, 1991, p. 3.

12. ———, "2 Kings Compete for Holy Shrines," *New York Times*, May 14, 1992, p. 7; and "Still Reeling from the Gulf War, Jordanians Harden Attitudes," *New York Times*, June 14, 1992, p. 12.

13. Egyptians and Jordanians exchanged insults in their respective establishment newspapers through the summer of 1992. See, for example, Cairo's *Al-Akhbar*, July 10, 1992, as reported in FBIS-NES, July 15, 1992. In the autumn of 1992, however, Egyptian-Jordanian tensions began to ease; Jordan's King Hussein made a brief trip to Cairo in October and met with Egyptian President Hosni Mubarak.

14. Cairo Middle East News Agency (MENA), May 10, 1992, as reported in FBIS-NES, May 12, 1992.

15. A fact that is often forgotten is that Egypt and Syria sent troops to Kuwait in 1961 in the aftermath of Iraq's threats to take over that newly independent state.

16. See Mubarak's interview in *Sawt al-Kuwayt al-Duwali*, September 19, 1991, as reported in FBIS-NES, September 23, 1991.

17. Cairo MENA, May 11, 1992, as reported in FBIS-NES, May 12, 1992.

18. Egypt and Syria deployed 30,000 and 17,000 troops to Saudi Arabia, respectively, during Desert Shield. The United States sent approximately 500,000 troops to Saudi Arabia and the Persian Gulf. For figures on the Arab troop deployment, see Bruce Maddy-Weizmann, *The Inter-Arab System and the Gulf War: Continuity and Change*, Carter Center of Emory University Occasional Paper, vol. 2, no. 1 (Atlanta, 1992), p. 16.

19. Youssef Ibrahim, "54 Qatar Citizens Petition Emir for Free Elections," *New York Times*, May 13, 1992, p. 15.

20. Sayigh, "The Gulf Crisis," p. 488.

21. On April 7, 1992, Saudi Defense Minister Sultan Bin Abd-al-Aziz al Saud stated: "Cooperation is complete among the states in the region, especially with the brothers in Egypt and Syria, and with the Gulf States." (FBIS-NES, April 8, 1992.)

22. See London's *Sawt al-Kuwait al-Duwali*, July 21, 1992, as reported in FBIS-NES, July 23, 1992.

23. Damascus Syrian Arab Television Network, June 3, 1992, as reported in FBIS-NES, June 4, 1992.

24. Cairo ESC (Egyptian Satellite Channel) Television, July 18, 1992, as reported in FBIS-NES, July 20, 1992.

25. Ibid.

26. See the remarks of Saudi Foreign Minister Faysal in Riyadh SPA, July 24, 1992, as reported in FBIS-NES, July 27, 1992.

27. Saudi Foreign Minister Faysal, representing the GCC states, attended the July 1992 meeting in Damascus on Arab coordination in the peace process.

28. Many Arab intellectuals believe that the Arab states have abandoned the plight of Palestinian refugees in the aftermath of the Gulf crisis. Elsayed Yassin, director of the Arab Thought Forum in Amman, Jordan, stated: "One byproduct of the Gulf war is that the Gulf countries have distanced themselves from the Palestinian problem, leaving the Jordanians and the Palestinians alone to face the situation." As quoted in Ibrahim, "Still Reeling from the Gulf War."

29. As quoted in Jackson Diehl, "'New Reality' Palestinians Embrace Diplomacy," *Washington Post*, October 24, 1991, pp. 41, 45.

30. Ibid.

31. For example, after an Arab coordination meeting on the peace process in Damascus in late July 1992, Syrian Foreign Minister Farouk Shara stated: "The Arab parties affirm their support for the peace process and their readiness to resume bilateral talks as soon as possible." But he added that the Arab ministers "found that the new Israeli Government has not so far, despite the change of tone and style, expressed its commitment for establishing a just, comprehensive and permanent peace in the region." As quoted in "Arab Foreign Ministers Support Mideast Talks," *New York Times*, July 26, 1992, p. 15.

32. As quoted in Chris Hedges, "Arabs Meeting in Syria Bar Separate Deals with Israel, *New York Times*, October 25, 1991, p. 8.

33. Cairo MENA, July 30, 1992, as reported in FBIS-NES, July 31, 1992.

34. The Syrians had negotiated indirectly with the Israelis, through U.S. mediation, to achieve a disengagement agreement for the Golan Heights, but had not agreed to participate in a U.S.-brokered peace process until the Madrid conference in 1991. Syria, for example, did not attend the short-lived Geneva conference, sponsored by the United States and the Soviet Union, after the 1973 Arab-Israeli war.
35. Cairo's *Rose Al-Yusuf*, April 6, 1992, as reported in FBIS-NES, April 15, 1992.
36. Arab Republic of Egypt Radio Network, June 3, 1992, as reported in FBIS-NES, June 4, 1992.
37. Interviews with several Arab intellectuals during a trip to the region in February 1992.
38. See the article by Mahmoud Abd-al-Munim Murad in Cairo's *Al-Akhbar*, April 2, 1992, as reported in FBIS-NES, April 8, 1992.

CHAPTER 3

1. Hrair Dekmejian, *Egypt under Nasser* (Albany, N.Y.: State University of New York Press, 1971), p. 106.
2. Ali Dessouki, "The New Arab Political Order," in Malcolm H. Kerr and El Sayed Yassin, eds., *Rich and Poor States in the Middle East: Egypt and the New Arab Order* (Boulder, Colo.: Westview Press, 1982), p. 330.
3. Dekmejian, *Egypt under Nasser*, pp. 42–45 and 108–113.
4. Adeed Dawisha, *Egypt in the Arab World* (New York: John Wiley & Sons, 1976), p. 87.
5. Ibid., p. 88.
6. Yezid Sayigh, "The Gulf Crisis: Why the Arab Regional Order Failed," *International Affairs*, vol. 67, no. 3 (1991), p. 490.
7. Fouad Ajami, "Between Cairo and Damascus: The Arab World and the New Stalemate," *Foreign Affairs*, vol. 54, no. 3 (Spring 1976), p. 444.
8. Abdel Monem Said Aly, "Egypt: A Decade after Camp David," in William B. Quandt, ed., *The Middle East: Ten Years after Camp David* (Washington, D.C.: Brookings Institution, 1988), pp. 70–73.
9. William Quandt, who served as Middle East director in President Carter's National Security Council, has written: "President Sadat, who had little patience for economic discussions, seemed to assume that Washington would provide the solvent for his country's economic problems." See *The*

United States and Egypt (Washington, D.C.: Brookings Institution, 1990), p. 40.

10. See Aly, "Egypt: A Decade after Camp David," p. 73.

11. Ali E. Hillal Dessouki, "Egyptian Foreign Policy since Camp David," in Quandt, *The Middle East*, pp. 108–109.

12. See Mubarak's interview with London's *Sawt al-Kuwayt al-Duwali*, September 19, 1991, as reported in FBIS-NES, September 23, 1991. Bitterly recalling his meeting with Saddam Hussein in July 1990, Mubarak stated: "When I inquired about [Saddam's] troop movements before the invasion, he said to me, 'I will not do anything. This is enough.' "

13. Ann Lesch, "Contrasting Reactions to the Persian Gulf Crisis: Egypt, Syria, Jordan, and the Palestinians," *Middle East Journal*, vol. 45, no. 1 (Winter 1991), p. 49.

14. Mubarak explained that Saddam wanted to "usurp Egyptian leadership" of the Arab world, "an impossible thing" (*Al-Ahram*, September 28, 1990).

15. Bruce Maddy-Weizmann, *The Inter-Arab System and the Gulf War: Continuity and Change*, Carter Center of Emory University Occasional Paper, vol. 2, no. 1 (Atlanta, 1992), p. 14.

16. Dessouki, "Egyptian Foreign Policy since Camp David," p. 104.

17. Maddy-Weizmann, *The Inter-Arab System and the Gulf War*, p. 16.

18. See the interview with Egyptian Foreign Minister Musa in London's *Al-Sharq al-Awsat*, September 24, 1991, as reported in FBIS-NES, September 27, 1991.

19. London's *Sawt al-Kuwayt al-Duwali*, September 19, 1991, as reported in FBIS-NES, September 23, 1991.

20. Cairo MENA, March 4, 1992, as reported in FBIS-NES, March 4, 1992.

21. Arab Republic of Egypt Radio Network, October 15, 1991, as reported in FBIS-NES, October 17, 1991.

22. Cairo Egyptian Satellite Channel (ESC) Television, July 18, 1992, as reported in FBIS-NES, July 18, 1992.

23. London's *Al-Sharq al-Awsat*, September 24, 1991, as reported in FBIS-NES, September 27, 1991.

24. Cairo MENA, October 19, 1991, as reported in FBIS-NES, October 21, 1991.

25. Cairo *Al-Jumhuriyah*, June 25, 1992, as reported in FBIS-NES, July 7, 1992.

26. Jerusalem *Qol Yisrael*, April 17, 1992, as reported in FBIS-NES, April 22, 1992.

27. Arab Republic of Egypt Radio Network, February 21, 1992, as reported in FBIS-NES, February 26, 1992.

28. Arab Republic of Egypt Radio Network, March 21, 1992, as reported in FBIS-NES, March 23, 1992.

29. Cairo MENA, November 16, 1991, as reported in FBIS-NES, November 18, 1991.

30. Paris (Agence-France Press), November 17, 1991, as reported in FBIS-NES, November 18, 1991.

31. For example, Egypt's semiofficial *Al-Ahram* stated on March 3, 1992, that the United States "has rejected all mediation, shrugged off legalities, and dismissed compromise solutions that have been offered" (Cairo MENA, March 3, 1992, as reported in FBIS-NES, March 4, 1992).

32. Cairo MENA, April 15, 1992, as reported in FBIS-NES, April 16, 1992.

33. Chris Hedges, "On the Road to Tripoli: Expect a Detour," *New York Times*, April 15, 1992, p. 6

34. Patrick Tyler and Eric Schmitt, "Pentagon Charts Military Options for Bombing Iraq," *New York Times*, March 19, 1992, p. 15; see also Patrick Tyler, "Confronting Hussein: Risky for Bush," *New York Times*, March 20, 1992, p. 8.

35. *Al-Ahram Al-Masa'i*, July 25, 1992, as reported in FBIS-NES, July 31, 1992.

36. London's *Sawt al-Kuwayt al-Duwali*, September 19, 1991, as reported in FBIS-NES, September 23, 1991.

37. Arab Republic of Egypt Radio Network, June 1, 1992, as reported in FBIS-NES, June 13, 1992.

38. Cairo MENA, February 21, 1992, as reported in FBIS-NES, February 24, 1992.

39. Egypt has reassured Syria that it will not support any attempt to isolate the Golan Heights issue from the framework of the Arab-Israeli peace negotiations. See Cairo's *Al-Jumhuriyah*, June 25, 1992, as reported in FBIS-NES, July 7, 1992. Additionally, Egypt's *Al-Ahram* has supported Syrian protestations against Turkey over the latter's "dangerous" water policy. See Cairo MENA, July 26, 1992, as reported in FBIS-NES, July 29, 1992.

40. Sayigh, "The Gulf Crisis," p. 505

41. For the complete text of the Arab League Council resolutions, see Cairo MENA, September 14, 1992, as reported in FBIS-NES, September 15, 1992.

42. Cairo MENA, April 21, 1992, as reported in FBIS-NES, April 22, 1992.

43. Cairo MENA, April 11, 1992, as reported in FBIS-NES, April 14, 1992.

44. Patrick Tyler, "Saudi Arabia Pledges $1 Billion to Soviet Union," *New York Times*, October 9, 1991, p. 9.
45. Cairo MENA, April 11, 1992, as reported in FBIS-NES, April 14, 1992.
46. Mubarak told students and faculty of Alexandria University that the Egyptian army "has now been asked to join peace-keeping forces in a sensitive part of the world. This is a very great boost to our reputation." (Cairo ESC Television, July 18, 1992, as reported in FBIS-NES, July 20, 1992.)

CHAPTER 4

1. Ashraf Ghorbal, "A Look Ahead—Problems and Prospects," in Ibrahim M. Oweiss, ed., *The Political Economy of Contemporary Egypt* (Washington, D.C.: Center for Contemporary Arab Studies, 1990), p. 309.
2. See the box "Key Facts" in the *Financial Times* survey on Egypt, January 21, 1992, section III, p. VI.
3. Chris Hedges, "After the Earthquake, a Rumbling of Discontent," *New York Times*, October 21, 1992, p. 4; and Carol Berger, "Protests Mount in Egypt over Pace of Quake Relief," *Christian Science Monitor*, October 20, 1992, p. 6.
4. Cairo ESC Television, July 18, 1992, as reported in FBIS-NES, July 20, 1992.
5. Cairo MENA, December 10, 1991, as reported in FBIS-NES, December 11, 1991.
6. Ali E. Hillal Dessouki, "The Primacy of Economics: The Foreign Policy of Egypt," in Baghat Korany and Ali E. Hillal Dessouki, eds., *The Foreign Policies of Arab States* (Boulder, Colo., and London: Westview Press, 1984), p. 124.
7. *Middle East Economic Digest*, vol. 36, no. 14 (April 10, 1992), p. 13; and Tony Walker, "The Medicine Seems to Be Working," *Financial Times*, January 21, 1992, section III, p. 3. Higher world oil prices in 1990 also helped to improve Egypt's balance of payments.
8. Some scholars and journalists estimate it at 20 percent. See Yahya M. Sadowski, *Political Vegetables? Businessman and Bureaucrat in the Development of Egyptian Agriculture* (Washington, D.C.: Brookings Institution, 1991), p. 22; and Chris Hedges, "Domestic Problems Hurt Rising Stature of Egypt," *New York Times*, July 12, 1992, p. 6.
9. Interview with an academic expert in Cairo, February 1992.
10. Sadowski, *Political Vegetables?* p. 22.

11. Cairo ESC Television, July 18, 1992, as reported in FBIS-NES, July 20, 1992.
12. *Al-Ahram*, February 7–8, 1992.
13. Cairo MENA, May 1, 1992, as reported in FBIS-NES, May 5, 1992.
14. Cairo MENA, June 8, 1992, as reported in FBIS-NES, June 11, 1992.
15. *Al-Ahram*, February 7–8, 1992.
16. Tony Walker, "The Medicine Seems to Be Working," *Financial Times*, January 12, 1992, section III, p. III.
17. Cairo *Al-Ahram Al-Duwali*, June 6, 1992, as reported in *Egypt: Economic Review*, no. 2, FBIS, July 7, 1992.
18. For example, on June 25, 1992, officials of Egypt and the Kuwaiti Fund for Economic Development signed an accord for the construction of a power station in Egypt, costing 44 million Kuwaiti dinars. (Cairo Egyptian Satellite Channel, June 25, 1992, as reported in FBIS-NES, June 30, 1992.) Moreover, in late 1991 the United Arab Emirates agreed to finance a project designed to reclaim 40,000 feddans of land east of Suez. (Cairo MENA, December 10, 1991, as reported in FBIS-NES, December 11, 1991.)
19. Cairo MENA, September 18, 1991, as reported in FBIS-NES, September 20, 1991.
20. For a discussion of the bureaucratic problems that foreign investors faced, see Nazih N. M. Ayubi, "Implementation Capability and Political Feasibility of the Open Door Policy in Egypt," in Malcolm H. Kerr and El Sayed Yassin, eds., *Rich and Poor States in the Middle East: Egypt and the New Arab Order* (Boulder, Colo.: Westview Press, 1982), pp. 374–379.
21. John Waterbury, a prominent scholar on the political economy of Egypt, has written: "Foreign investment has been below what had been forecast, and most of it has been concentrated in financial services. When that kind of investment is netted out, Law 43 [foreign investment] flows have accounted for only 7 percent of gross fixed investment over the period 1974–79." See "The 'Soft State' and the Open Door: Egypt's Experience with Economic Liberalization, 1974–84," *Comparative Politics*, vol. 18, no. 1 (October 1985), p. 76.
22. Ayubi, "Implementation Capability," p. 362. In 1979 total Arab investments in Egyptian banks were estimated at $4 billion.
23. Mubarak admitted in an interview that investors "used to come and shortly afterwards used to go away saying there is

no hope." See Cairo's *Sabah al-Khayr*, September 19, 1991, as reported in FBIS-NES, September 25, 1991.

24. Interview with an academic expert in Cairo, February 1992. Higher interest rates in Egyptian banks, however, have led some private Egyptian businessmen with capital outside the country to begin to place some of their funds in the Egyptian banking system.

25. Ibrahim Saad Eddine Abdallah, "Migration as a Factor Conditioning State Economic Control and Financial Policy Options," in Giacomo Luciani and Ghassan Salame, eds., *The Politics of Arab Integration* (London: Croom Helm, 1988), p. 141.

26. In 1983 officially recorded remittances from Egyptian workers totaled $3.3 billion, equivalent to the combined revenues of Egypt's oil exports and Suez canal tolls. See Sadowski, *Political Vegetables?* pp. 84–85.

27. Abdallah, "Migration," p. 140.

28. "Foreign Labor Trends: Egypt," (Cairo: U.S. Embassy, 1991).

29. Ahmad al-Imawi, chairman of the Egyptian General Trade Union Federation, cited this figure. See Cairo MENA, April 12, 1992, as reported in FBIS, April 13, 1992. Many Egyptians are gainfully employed in Libya's expanded agricultural sector, while others are merely pursuing marginal work, such as selling Egyptian goods on the street. Some have probably returned to Egypt since the spring of 1992, so the actual figure may now be closer to 1.0 million. Although many Egyptian workers in Libya are not pursuing full-time jobs, their presence in Libya alleviates an economic burden for the Egyptian government.

30. Ghada Hashem Talhami, *Palestine and Egyptian National Identity* (New York: Praeger, 1992), p. 34.

31. See Leonard Binder, *In a Moment of Enthusiasm* (Chicago: University of Chicago Press, 1979).

32. This action prompted Egyptian Interior Minister Musa to state, "What is this becoming, a state within a state?" As quoted in Hedges, "After the Earthquake."

33. For example, on May 7, 1992, the Muslim Brotherhood condemned sectarian clashes in Upper Egypt that were widely believed to have been fomented by the Gama'at. (Paris AFP, May 8, 1992, as reported in FBIS, May 8, 1992.)

34. On January 31, 1992, Mubarak stated that he would not overturn the verdict of an Egyptian author who was sentenced to eight years in prison for blasphemy. See *Al-Wafd*,

February 1, 1992, as reported in FBIS-NES, February 5, 1992.

35. Two months later, however, Mubarak came out against public executions. See Cairo MENA, April 2, 1992, as reported in FBIS-NES, April 3, 1992.

36. John Waterbury, *The Egypt of Nasser and Sadat: The Political Economy of Two Regimes* (Princeton: Princeton University Press, 1983), p. 244.

37. Ibid., p. 242.

38. Talhami, *Palestine and Egyptian National Identity*, p. 159.

39. The Egyptian political system under Mubarak cannot be considered a democracy in the Western parliamentary sense, because it retains aspects of authoritarian rule and restricts some civil liberties. Nonetheless, Mubarak has allowed a relatively free press to flourish, and Egyptian intellectuals and opposition politicians frequently and openly criticize government policies.

40. Arab Republic of Egypt Radio Network, April 30, 1992, as reported in FBIS-NES, May 5, 1992.

41. Cairo *Sabah Al-Khayr*, September 19, 1991, as reported in FBIS-NES, September 25, 1991.

42. Chris Hedges, "Opinions of Arabs Are Ranging Even to Indifference," *New York Times*, November 1, 1991, p. 9; and Cairo MENA, October 30, 1991, as reported in FBIS-NES, October 31, 1991.

43. Cairo *Al-Shab*, October 29, 1991, as reported in FBIS-NES, November 5, 1991.

44. Cairo ESC, November 3, 1991, as reported in FBIS-NES, November 5, 1991.

45. Cairo MENA, June 6, 1992, as reported in FBIS-NES, June 9, 1992.

46. Cairo MENA, October 19, 1991, as reported in FBIS-NES, October 21, 1991.

47. As quoted in Thomas L. Friedman, "Amid Histrionics, Arabs and Israelis Team Up to Lose an Opportunity," *New York Times*, November 3, 1991, section IV, pp. 1, 4.

48. This message was emphasized in Musa's address to the United Nations on September 30, 1991. See the text of his address in FBIS-NES, October 1, 1991.

49. Cairo MENA, July 5, 1992, as reported in FBIS-NES, July 6, 1992.

50. *Al-Ahram* called for the lifting of economic sanctions in July; Mubarak made a statement to the same effect in August.

51. Youssef Ibrahim, "The Arabs Find a World in Which They Count Less," *New York Times*, April 5, 1992, p. E3.
52. Ibid.
53. Arab Republic of Egypt Radio Network, April 16, 1992, as reported in FBIS-NES, April 17, 1992.
54. Tripoli JANA, May 27, 1992, as reported in FBIS-NES, May 28, 1992.

CHAPTER 5

1. William B. Quandt, *The United States and Egypt* (Washington, D.C.: Brookings Institution, 1990), p. 2.
2. See Hermann Frederick Eilts, "The United States and Egypt," in William B. Quandt, ed., *The Middle East: Ten Years after Camp David* (Washington, D.C.: Brookings Institution, 1988), pp. 126–128.
3. Ali E. Hillal Dessouki, "The Primacy of Economics: The Foreign Policy of Egypt," in Baghat Korany and Ali E. Hillal Dessouki, eds., *The Foreign Policies of Arab States* (Boulder, Colo., and London: Westview Press, 1984), pp. 128–130.
4. Ibid., p. 129.
5. Ali E. Hillal Dessouki, "Egyptian Foreign Policy since Camp David," in Quandt, *The Middle East*, pp. 106–107.
6. Saad Eddin Ibrahim, "Domestic Developments in Egypt," in Quandt, *The Middle East*, p. 27.
7. Dessouki, "Egyptian Foreign Policy since Camp David," p. 105.
8. Ibrahim, "Domestic Developments in Egypt," p. 28.
9. Cairo MENA, June 8, 1992, as reported in FBIS-NES, June 11, 1992.
10. Cairo *Al-Ahram Weekly*, July 2–8, 1992, as reported in FBIS-NES, July 9, 1992.
11. Interview with an Egyptian intellectual in Cairo, February 1992.
12. Cairo *Al-Ahram Weekly*, July 2–8, 1992, as reported in FBIS-NES, July 9, 1992.
13. Cairo MENA, July 8, 1992, as reported in FBIS-NES, July 9, 1992.
14. Mubarak explained that Saddam Hussein wanted to usurp Egyptian leadership of the Arab world, "an impossible thing." See *Al-Ahram*, September 20, 1991. See also Ann Lesch, "Contrasting Reactions to the Persian Gulf Crisis: Egypt, Syria, Jordan, and the Palestinians," *Middle East Journal*, vol. 45, no. 1 (Winter 1991), p. 49.

15. *Al-Ahram*, June 30, 1992, as reported in FBIS-NES, July 7, 1992.
16. Michael Wines, "U.S. Will Try Diplomatic Actions Before a Military strike on Libya," *New York Times*, November 16, 1991, p. 4; see also Paris Radio Monte Carlo, November 17, 1991, as reported in FBIS-NES, November 18, 1991.
17. For example, one Egyptian writer stated in a government-owned newspaper that the United States "has enough votes at the Security Council to pass any resolution to punish, besiege, or discipline whoever it wants, which is exactly what is happening to Libya today." From an article by Kamal 'Abd-al-Ra'uf in *Akhbar al-Yawm*, April 4, 1992, as reported in FBIS-NES, April 15, 1992.
18. Patrick Tyler and Eric Schmitt, "Pentagon Charts Military Options for Bombing Iraq," *New York Times*, March 19, 1992, p. 15.
19. Cairo MENA, March 14, 1992, as reported in FBIS-NES, March 17, 1992.
20. Cairo MENA, October 19, 1991, as reported in FBIS-NES, October 21, 1991.
21. An unnamed Egyptian diplomat stated in November 1991: "I think the Syrians are wasting a lot of energy over meaningless details. . . . Since the talks have started and the Syrians have participated, we should facilitate the putting of pressure by Washington on Israel instead of quarreling over procedural matters of little importance." As quoted in Youssef Ibrahim, "Arabs Split on Strategy for Next Round of Talks," *New York Times*, November 26, 1991, p. 10.
22. Interview with Egyptian Foreign Minister Musa in London's *Al-Hayah*, November 2, 1991, as reported in FBIS-NES, November 6, 1991.
23. London's *Al-Hawadith*, February 28, 1992, as reported in FBIS-NES, March 4, 1992. See also Tel Aviv's *Davar*, May 11, 1992, as reported in FBIS-NES, May 11, 1992.
24. Jerusalem Israel Television Network, July 21, 1992, as reported in FBIS-NES, July 23, 1992.
25. Cairo MENA, July 13, 1992, as reported in FBIS-NES, July 14, 1992.
26. Cairo MENA, February 21, 1992, as reported in FBIS-NES, February 24, 1992.
27. Sadat once said the he preferred "action to reaction." As quoted in Dessouki, "The Primacy of Economics," p. 133.

28. As quoted in Youssef Ibrahim, "Can Egypt Bring Israelis and Arabs Together?" *New York Times*, July 26, 1992, section IV, pp. 1–2.

29. Paris AFP in English, as reported in FBIS-NES, July 20, 1992.

30. Egyptian Foreign Minister Musa, quoted in Cairo MENA February 21, 1992, as reported in FBIS-NES, February 24, 1992. Musa also agreed with an interviewer's statement that "nothing short of Syrian sovereignty will be accepted." See London's *Al-Sharq al-Awsat*, July 16, 1992, as reported in FBIS-NES, July 20, 1992.

31. Mubarak advisor Osama al-Baz stated that Egypt welcomed the idea of a meeting of Arab foreign ministers involved in the peace process and was "one of the parties that sought to convene such a meeting." (Cairo MENA, July 19, 1992, as reported in FBIS-NES, July 20, 1992.)

32. Tel Aviv's *Al Hamishmar*, July 22, 1992, as reported in FBIS-NES, July 22, 1992.

33. For example, Sadat once described the Soviets as "crude and tasteless people." As quoted in Dessouki, "The Primacy of Economics," p. 129.

34. Egypt's bitter experience with British imperialism is still in evidence on a cultural level. The Egyptian-run museum at El Alamein, supposedly built to commemorate the famous World War II battle, is as much an indictment of colonialism as it is a story of the actual battle. The museum houses a model of the large British barracks of Kasr el-Nil in central Cairo, which, the caption tells viewers, was torn down after the 1952 revolution. Another caption tells viewers that Egypt did not take part in the battle of El Alamein because the British prevented Egypt from having anything more than a "toy army."

35. Seth Faison, "UN Chief Mired in Dispute With Security Council," *New York Times*, July 24, 1992, p. 3. Boutros Ghali, responding to British press criticism he received over this controversy, wondered in an interview if it was "because I'm a wog," a derogatory word from the nineteenth century that the British used to describe their colonial subjects. See Patrick Tyler, "UN Chief's Dispute With Council Boils Over," *New York Times*, August 3, 1992, pp. 1, 9.

36. Quandt, *The United States and Egypt*, p. 6.

37. For Egyptian complaints about the nature and extent of U.S. economic assistance, see Eilts, "The United States and Egypt," pp. 136–139.

38. Hugh Carnegy, "U.S. Assistance Far from Trouble Free," *Financial Times*, January 21, 1992, section III, p. III.
39. Cairo MENA, June 8, 1992, as reported in FBIS-NES, June 11, 1992.
40. Chris Hedges, "Domestic Problems Hurt Rising Stature of Egypt," *New York Times*, July 12, 1992, p. 6.
41. Maurice Makramallah, Egypt's minister of state for international cooperation, said optimistically that the investment accord "will provide Egypt with the financial resources it needs to finance the economic development projects." He added that the U.S. investor will bring modern technology to Egypt and will provide job opportunities for Egyptian workers (Cairo MENA, May 28, 1992, as reported in FBIS-NES, June 2, 1992).
42. Mubarak gave the following breakdown of total investment in Egypt by nationality: Egyptian, 70 percent; Arab, 17–18 percent; and foreign (non-Arab), 2–3 percent. (Speech at Alexandria University in Cairo ESC Television, July 18, 1992, as reported in FBIS-NES, July 20, 1992.)
43. Saudi Arabia's commerce minister stated that Saudi businessmen have expressed an interest in investing in Egypt and entering into joint ventures. His Egyptian counterpart noted that trade relations between the two countries were expanding. See Riyadh SPA, February 18, 1992, as reported in FBIS-NES, February 24, 1992.
44. Quandt, *The United States and Egypt*, pp. 28–29.
45. Ibid., p. 6.
46. Cairo MENA, June 8, 1992, as reported in FBIS-NES, June 11, 1992.

INDEX